Praise for Stephen Russell Payne and

Riding My Guitar – The Rick Norcross Story

"In RIDING MY GUITAR – THE RICK NORCROSS STORY, author Stephen Russell Payne tells an engaging tale of an authentic Vermont talent who might otherwise have remained below the national radar. Rick Norcross's gifts as a songwriter, performer, and photographer are eclipsed only by his generosity and warmth."

— George Thomas, longtime Vermont Public Radio music host

"Stephen Russell Payne has emerged as a new voice in Vermont's impressive pantheon of creative writers, and a powerful one. For years I've enjoyed his journalism and short fiction. Now with his new book, Payne has shown Rick Norcross to be a true Vermont original, a kind of musical Jack Kerouac. RIDING MY GUITAR – THE RICK NORCROSS STORY perfectly captures his talent, his history, and his good heart."

— Howard Frank Mosher, award winning author

"RIDING MY GUITAR – THE RICK NORCROSS STORY is the entertaining story of a true Vermont original. Rick Norcross's amazing journey has taken him throughout the U.S. and to Europe, but at heart he remains a friendly, modest and very talented Vermonter. In telling this story of the irrepressible Norcross, Stephen Payne also gives us a vivid picture of rural Vermont in the 1950's and '60's. It's a fun read!"

— Tom Slayton, Editor Emeritus, Vermont Life Magazine

"Stephen Russell Payne's short stories have shown him to be among New England's finest writers of regional fiction."

— X. J. Kennedy, award winning poet and editor

"No one writes with as much passion and insight about northern Vermont as Stephen Russell Payne. With the meticulousness of a surgeon, and the lyricism of a poet, Payne captures the tenacity and honesty of the denizens of the Green Mountain State's small towns and villages. Reading Payne is like a visit from a good old friend. His tales are always infused with equal measures of humor, wisdom, and love."

— Jennifer Finney Boylan, best selling author

For Frank Ittleman with great respect and affection over many years, Very Best, Steve

RIDING MY GUITAR

The Rick Norcross Story

STEPHEN RUSSELL PAYNE

2013

Cedar Ledge Publishing

ISBN 13: 9781482529272
ISBN 10: 1482529270

Manufactured in the United States of America

For information, permissions and appearances, please visit our website,
www.StephenRussellPayne.com or facebook at Stephen Russell Payne.

Cedar Ledge Publishing
Burlington, Vermont 05401

For my friend,
Jonathan Edwards
One of America's great troubadours

Your songs, support, and personal kindnesses
Have made such a difference,
And for that, I am deeply grateful.

ACKNOWLEDGEMENTS

I want to thank the many people who graciously and generously gave their time to help me research this complex story. Through interviews, emails, phone calls, and over countless cups of coffee, the following people helped me come to understand the deep and fascinating fabric of Rick Norcross's life.

Hugh and Nancy Aldous, Harry Atkinson, Barb Bardin, Becky Blanchard, Matt Bushlow, Mark Bushnell, Bret Corbin, Jack Donovan, Dan Dubonnet, Rosie Flores, Kathleen Gill, Cathy Gillespie, Ken Grillo, Julia Shannon-Grillo, Carolyn Hester, Brett Hoffman, Nancy Johnson, Abby Kaighin, Captain J.A. Lewis, Charlie MacFadyen, Lois McClure, Holly Miller, Taryn Noelle, LeRoy Preston, The Legendary Panama Red, Dave Rowell, Leo Roy, Elaine Russell, Joan Shannon, Frank Ross, Derek Sarjeant, Susan Eastman Slayton, Creighton Smith, Ken Squier, George Thomas, and Lorraine Patch Zigman.

I want to thank greenmountainphotography.com for permission to use their photograph of Rick for the cover. The back cover author photograph is by Natalie Stultz. Photographs in the center section were kindly supplied by Rick Norcross except as noted in captions.

I also want to extend heartfelt appreciation to my wife, Marietta, my talented and tireless *First Reader*, and to my longtime editor, Lesley Kellas Payne of Fresno, California. And finally, many thanks to the one and only Rick Norcross for giving me the privilege and pleasure of writing this book, an adventure I'll never forget.

INTRODUCTION

As a writer who grew up in the heart of Vermont's Northeast Kingdom, I am always looking for new stories to tell about unique Vermont characters. The day I met Rick Norcross I felt like I had discovered the *Mother Lode*. I'd known of Rick as a musician for many years, had enjoyed hearing his band, the Ramblers, but had never met him until one day in the summer of 2010. I had just finished editing my novel, *Cliff Walking*, and was in Burlington relaxing on the waterfront when I saw Rick and the Ramblers' bright green, 1957 Flxible Starliner tour bus parked in the railroad yard next to Perkins Pier. Intrigued by the classic old bus, I decided to research Rick and his band.

I soon contacted Rick, and he invited me to visit him at his remarkable home and museum, Rambler Ranch, just across the street from the bus. He was warm and welcoming, and very enthusiastic that I might be interested in writing about his life and, most importantly, about his beloved band. "Where've you been all these years?" he asked with a grin. We talked for several hours then headed to the nearby Shanty Restaurant and that's when I learned if I was going to be successful writing about Rick Norcross, *lunch* needed to be mentioned on a regular basis. Satisfying that man's appetite turned out to be the secret to him revealing his fascinating life story.

Fortunately for me, Rick had methodically archived the vast majority of his life's journey, filling his home – including a huge multi-drawer nautical chart chest — with memorabilia from his earliest days in East Hardwick, to his childhood living at the Shelburne Museum, and his musical tours of Florida, England, Europe, and everywhere in between. His spirited life and career are a tapestry of music, photography and writings about his own times and the stories of others. They are filled with outrageous humor, difficult and trying interludes, and just enough triumphs to keep it all going. The number of people Rick Norcross has touched and have touched him is truly astounding. In remarkable ways, over 50 years after he first started playing a guitar, he continues to leave his unique mark on the world.

Rick and I spent hundreds of hours together working through the details of his life and, in so doing, inevitably became friends. The February after we met, he came to a winter party at our house and offered to perform a few songs after dinner. Wielding his guitar and sharp sense of humor, he spontaneously entertained a room full of people for an hour, leaving them laughing and asking for more. What struck me most about that evening was that my teenage children and their friends were as riveted by Rick's performance as everyone else in the room and, in this techno-texting age that is not easy to do.

In March of 2011, Rick traveled to Tampa, Florida, to perform a concert in the city where he spent many years as a singer-songwriter and journalist. I had made plans to fly down for the show, but developed pneumonia a few days before I was to leave. Nonetheless, I got on the plane and when I stepped out of the terminal into the warm Florida sunshine, I found Rick waiting in his convertible, top down and a cooler of fresh-squeezed orange juice on my seat. I was touched by his kindness, and it was the best tasting OJ I'd ever had.

Over the next two days, Rick drove me all over Tampa, showing me the haunts he frequented in the 1970's, including the Ybor City neighborhood where he bought a house next to an elderly Spaniard, Mr. Pepine, who in the 1950's, lunched every day with Fidel Castro. Rick brought the history of Tampa alive and was a most entertaining guide. At his solo concert that Sunday afternoon, he entertained the audience royally, personally passing out Lake Champlain Chocolates to every person in the audience.

Rick's music and the people he has shared it with have always been the most important parts of his life. Though he has often struggled financially, he has done whatever it took to keep the music alive, including becoming a renowned Rock and Roll photographer and journalist during his five year stint working for the *Tampa Times*. Rick is also a folk historian chronicling Vermont's unique history through his original songs. Readers will learn never before told stories about the Green Mountain State as well as tales from his many years on the road performing.

I have come to respect and admire this man who, perhaps more than anyone else I've ever known, has marched only to the beat of his own drum — regardless of how difficult, at times, that has been. Delving deeply into a man's professional and personal life can be a treacherous undertaking and Rick has been generous in opening his head, heart and home to me. Though we have had some testy moments and a few minor writer-subject skirmishes, this has been a fascinating journey. I think at times both he and I felt insecure - him about revealing too much, me about not presenting his story in quite the right way. In the end, I know that researching and writing *Riding My Guitar - The Rick Norcross Story* is something for which I will always be grateful. I hope Rick's story will be as meaningful and entertaining for you to read as it has been for me to write.

PRELUDE

On a hot, sweaty night in September of 1970, inside Tampa, Florida's largest concert hall, 7,000 wildly enthusiastic fans waited for the King to appear. Feeling the press of the jam-packed, screaming crowd, Rick Norcross hunkered down in front of the stage, his camera equipment tucked under his seat out of sight. Elvis' manager, Colonel Parker, had imposed a strict photography blackout during the tour, but Rick was hoping his friends working security would let him get a few shots of the world's greatest superstar.

Sitting next to Rick was a photographer on assignment from the *New York Times*. When Rick saw the large flash bulb on the man's camera, he knew there would be trouble. Suddenly, two of Tampa's finest descended on the New York photographer. Rick crouched down as the burly officers each grabbed an arm of the man and yanked him out of his seat. Camera equipment flying about his neck, the man was quickly ejected through a nearby exit. Staying low, Rick glanced around the room. Though the place was ringed with cops, none of them were headed in his direction. Being a respected local music writer and photographer for the *Tampa Times*, he was pretty sure they would leave him alone. And, thankfully, they did.

Moments later, the house lights dimmed as brilliant spotlights flooded the stage. With his tremendous band rising to a crescendo, a smiling Elvis strode onto the stage in a white bell-bottomed jumpsuit, his high, crisp collar open down to his fine-toned abs. For a few moments Rick just stared up at the King who, with his endearing smile and captivating voice, was even more powerful in person than Rick had imagined. "He looked *so* good," Rick told me, "I felt like I was in the presence of royalty."

Just a few feet in front of Rick, Elvis grabbed hold of the chrome microphone stand and launched into a gyrating rendition of "That's All Right, Mama," at which point thousands of screaming girls leapt from their seats. Elvis began twisting his way back and forth across the stage, but despite the excitement Rick — ever the professional — focused on the job at hand. He raised his camera and brought Elvis into focus, the King so close his sweat dotted Rick's vest. Shooting with fast film in only the existing light, Rick proceeded to capture a collection of rare candid images of the King of Rock and Roll at the height of his career.

After the show, Rick slid out of the hall and made it back to the *Tampa Times* newsroom, where he wrote his review of one of the biggest musical events ever to hit Tampa. When his article ran the next afternoon, readers were struck by the beauty of Rick's photographs. As he would do with hundreds of concerts over the years, this young man from New England had captured a key piece of America's musical history, both in his enduring words and his poignant images.

The next night Rick returned to his first love, playing his own music at the area's longest running coffeehouse, Beaux Arts in nearby Pinellas Park, Florida. A well-known singer in his own right, audiences loved Rick's original comedic folk songs as much as he enjoyed playing them. From his humble beginnings in the tiny northern Vermont towns of his childhood to the bustling scenes of Tampa, and his own folk tours of England and Europe in between, Rick Norcross was living his dream. Half a century later, as longtime leader of Vermont's, Rick and the All-Star Ramblers Western Swing Band, he continues to entertain people of all ages with his music and inspire them with his remarkable life story.

Chapter One

I *CAME TO* IN VERMONT

Though it is painful for him to admit, Rick Norcross isn't quite a native Vermonter, though he's about as close as you can get. He was born on March 23, 1945 at a military hospital in Waltham, Massachusetts, where his father was stationed with the Army. Shortly thereafter, his father moved the family to his native Hardwick, Vermont, a tiny granite quarry town of about 2000 inhabitants on the western edge of what's known as the Northeast Kingdom. Rick likes to say, "Technically, I might have been born in Massachusetts, but I *came to* in Vermont!"

For the first few years of his life, Rick Norcross and his family lived with his paternal grandmother, Delilah Libby, the head nurse at the local hospital. Known for its winding rivers, strong-armed stone cutters and serious baseball and amateur boxing leagues, Hardwick of the 1940's was a tough community where working your fingers to the bone was considered essential for survival. Rick's grandmother came to Hardwick from Houlton, Maine, in 1901 after she graduated from nursing school. Situated in a remote northeast part of Maine, Houlton was known as the "Potato Capital," where schools shut down for two weeks during the annual potato harvest. Houlton was also the northern origin of the original US Route One, which ran south down the eastern face of America, all the way to Key West, Florida.

In those days, young nursing graduates were assigned to a particular case, which meant moving to a town that had a homebound patient in need of a nurse. Delilah's case was an elderly fellow named Norcross, who lived in Dow's Crossing in Walden, Vermont. As was the custom, Delilah moved into a room in the patient's house and began work as a private duty nurse. Before long, she met her patient's grandson, Ray Norcross, a spirited young farmer, who was said to be a "dashing figure" when riding his motorcycle. After a short courtship, Delilah and Ray married and moved to East Hardwick village, where he took over the town's barber shop, complete with two chrome-appointed leather chairs, a wide-mouthed spittoon and a heavy wooden pool table in the back, its felt worn thin from decades of keen competition.

Ray was a strapping young fellow, well known as a tough and talented pitcher for Hardwick Academy and later for the local granite companies' baseball teams. Baseball was a very popular spectator sport in the area and the players tended to be remarkably talented. So much so that even a Japanese team once came to Hardwick to play against them. Ray was one of Hardwick's best pitchers; that is, when he was sober enough to throw straight. Large crowds came out to watch him pitch and were known to repeatedly yell, "Go Norky!" to urge him on when on the verge of a strikeout.

Despite the fact that Ray lived during Prohibition and under the watchful, frowning eyes of the local Women's Christian Temperance Union, he was able to find enough homemade moonshine to keep him well lubricated much of the time. It was said that on occasion, after celebrating a baseball victory, Ray's buddies would mount him on his Indian motorcycle and give him a good shove in the direction of East Hardwick, and he would somehow find his way home.

Rick's father, Dean Hatfield Norcross, was born to Delilah and Ray in 1917. Unfortunately, Ray continued his hard drinking ways and was only in his mid twenties when he died of what Rick describes as "bad liquor." At the time no one knew if he'd died of poisoning from the lead solder used to construct local stills or, as his grandmother suspected, someone (perhaps an opposing pitcher?) had deliberately poisoned him. Regardless, by then Ray was well on the way to ruining his liver from drinking. For Delilah, losing her young husband in such a fashion left her dead set against all forms of the evil spirits, and she never again let anyone into her home who ingested so much as a single swallow of liquor. Years later that turned out to be a blessing for Rick, who somehow managed to avoid the deadly culture of alcohol and drugs that claimed the lives of so many aspiring young musicians in the 1960's and 1970's.

Growing up, Rick's father turned into quite the jokester and by his senior year in high school was a true hellion. The most memorable of his exploits was a day in 1936 when he lit Hardwick's Main Street on fire. Rick recalled what he was told years later by retired road superintendent, Frankie Russell, a crusty old fellow who lived two houses down from his grandmother. "It was the first time they paved Main Street and back then the process was to lay down a layer of crushed stone and then pass the town truck over it which then laid down a coat of hot tar. My father came out of Hardwick Academy to watch the men work and after the tar truck made its pass down the street, my father thought he'd liven things up so he struck a match and tossed it on the tar. People heard a massive whooshing sound as a sheet of flame burst into the air and swept down the street as the fumes above the hot tar burned off. It was a flash fire that quickly burned out without causing any real damage but my father got into *serious* trouble."

While Rick's father wasn't arrested, neither the local authorities, nor the townsfolk were the least bit amused by his dangerous prank. Rick continued, "That street fire gave those Hardwick folks quite a start. As punishment, for the next school term my father was sent by his family in his Model A over the mountain through Stannard every day to attend school at Lyndon Institute." Rick's father returned to Hardwick Academy to graduate with his Class of

1936. After that he left town, attended Green Mountain College in Poultney for one semester, then dropped out and enlisted in the Army.

When Rick was three, his father returned from a deployment in Germany and was stationed at Fort Ethan Allen in Colchester, Vermont. It was 1948, the Great War was over, and the fort had been turned into a depot for heavy weapons returning from the battlefields of Europe. Rick remembered playing by himself on the large parade field and watching dirigibles floating in the sky overhead, as well as the seemingly endless trainloads of Sherman tanks, field artillery, and howitzers arriving along the tracks behind Officers Row.

One of the good things about living at Fort Ethan Allen for Rick was a special next door neighbor named Mary Lee Banan, who was his mother's best friend. She was a beautiful young woman in her twenties, recently married to an Army sergeant stationed at the fort. Despite her close friendship with Rick and his family, Mary Lee never spoke of her life before coming to Vermont. It was many years later that Rick learned she was the very popular singer and movie star from the Gene Autry movies of the early 1940's.

While living at Fort Ethan Allen, each Sunday Rick's family headed off along Vermont's serpentine roads back to East Hardwick to visit Grammy Dell and other relatives. Rick enjoyed the outings, though it was usually quite an adventure getting there. "In those days the car trip on old Route 15 was so damn curvy that even the dog got sick." During the two hour drive, Rick's father would often let Rick and his sister stand up on the front seat of their '48 Dodge, bouncing up and down as they wound their way east following the picturesque Lamoille River. And, to the consternation of their mother, sometimes when they'd race over an old bridge, the kids would become airborne, banging their heads on the car roof. Rick thought that was great fun. "On those trips when we weren't car sick, we'd drive along with the windows down, wind blowing through the car, singing our favorite songs like, 'You Are My Sunshine' or 'Side by Side' at the top of our lungs."

Once in East Hardwick, Rick ran down to see his Great Aunt Susie and Uncle Phil who owned Eastman's General Store at the foot of the hill on the banks of the river. Rick would spend a few minutes leaning over the railing on the bridge, looking down at the swift, powerful current then run inside where Uncle Phil welcomed him from behind the counter. The store was filled with wonderful aromas from bins of cinnamon and other spices from the West Indies, along with barrels of milled grains and fresh pickles floating in thick brine. Leaning against the counter on the floor were gunny sacks of flour, sugar, rice and coffee beans. A faded checkerboard sat on an old table by the wood-stove in the middle of the scalloped, wide-planked floor. Shelves of canned and boxed goods lined the wall behind the broad wooden counter, and at one end there was a white, round-shouldered refrigerator filled with soda pop made at nearby Barr's Better Beverages. A special treat for visiting the store was Uncle Phil's offer of either a cold soda pop or a freshly made chocolate-covered marshmallow cookie. The cookies usually won out.

On the other side of the store was the East Hardwick Post Office, and Rick remembered marveling at how his Aunt could fit all the letters in those little metal boxes every day. Rick's cousin, Sukey, reminisced about the Eastmans living upstairs over the store. "To get up there was scary as a child as you had to enter a world of darkness and clutter which, if you were lucky, was lit by a single dull light bulb hanging from the high tin ceiling. In that corner of the building the oily smell of kerosene from the tanks below was nearly overwhelming. As you climbed, you had to feel your way along the stairs until you finally made it to the top where you were relieved to open the door into their brightly lit apartment and the smell of fresh-baked bread."

Over the years, visiting East Hardwick provided comfort, continuity, and grounding for Rick, as his own nuclear family descended into an increasingly anxiety-ridden atmosphere, the result of a badly strained marriage between his parents. His parents both came from broken homes, and his father, while he didn't light any more streets on fire, was a joker — about everything — making it nearly impossible to have a meaningful conversation with him. A regimented military man, he wasn't comfortable around kids and lacked the skills and interest to be an involved dad. Rick recalled that during those years there was never a time when he and his father tossed a ball, worked on a project together, went fishing, or even took a walk in the woods.

On the other hand, Rick's father was a skilled private pilot who loved to fly a buddy's small Cessna around the Lake Champlain Valley. He once took Rick's mother on a terrifying flight down to Bristol, Vermont, during which he allegedly "buzzed so low over the village cemetery she could read inscriptions on the monuments." Holding onto her seat with a death grip, she was so terrified she vowed she would never fly again."

Rick's mother grew up in an emotionally bitter family. When she was six years old, her father left her and her mother and headed to work in the wheat fields of Manitoba. They never saw him again. Rick described his maternal grandmother as an emotionally manipulative and bitter woman who hated men and passed on very limited parenting and communication skills to his mother. While at times his mother had a sense of humor and was supportive of Rick, much of his early upbringing was stressful and he did not always react well to it. "As a kid, I dealt with things by being a wiseass and thus was in some kind of minor trouble much of the time. And when a conversation wasn't going Mother's way or when she got mad at me, she would just stop talking – totally – sometimes for weeks at a time. There was just no negotiating with her when we were kids – about anything. Between her and my guilt-driven grandmother, we mostly walked on eggshells. I especially dreaded holidays because we were always trying not to offend anyone. If you did, it was the deafening silent treatment again. I didn't like being at home where I felt alone and very unhappy. Even when I was seven or eight I remember feeling like I couldn't wait to get out of there."

The sadness and disappointment surrounding his family situation was difficult for Rick. "My family wasn't evil in any way; my mom was very intelligent, honest and hard-working to a fault, but had little in the way of kid-rearing skills. I firmly believe she did the best she could with what she had and that was no training. She grew up with just a really grim mother, a Victorian woman who made life very hard for her."

Despite living in the beautiful, seemingly idyllic external landscape of the Green Mountain State, within Rick a storm of unease, fear and anxiety was developing. Though he found his way to a happy and fulfilled life through marvelous mentors, tenacious determination, and creativity, his family's dysfunction took a painful toll on many of his relationships. Though most everyone who knows Rick today, including Rick himself, would describe him as an eternal optimist, it is no small wonder given the difficulties he had to survive in his early life. And there were even more serious challenges to come.

Chapter Two

I RODE THE *TI*

Without much of any explanation, Rick's parents separated in 1951 when he was six. This coincided with his father leaving for a new US Army deployment in Formosa so Rick's mother moved him and his younger sister from Fort Ethan Allen to nearby Shelburne, Vermont. Shelburne was a small agricultural community where miles of fertile farmland stretched along the valley from the center of town to the shores of Lake Champlain. While the area was busier than East Hardwick, at that time the population was still small. Rick's class in the Shelburne elementary school had only 18 students, and all but five were farm kids. On the other hand, as provincial as Shelburne was, it was only a few miles up the road to the exciting Queen City of Burlington.

Rick's mother applied for a job at the Shelburne Museum, which was being expanded by its founder, wealthy New York socialite, Mrs. Electra Havemeyer Webb. Vermont had never seen anything quite like the "outdoor museum" Mrs. Webb was putting together on a gently sloping piece of farm land on the south end of town. An early aficionado of Americana and a serious collector of Impressionistic and other art forms, Mrs. Webb was in the process of moving to the museum grounds historically significant 18th and 19th Century buildings she had found in Shelburne and other nearby towns.

It was a very exciting time for the town as the museum had become an important new employer for the area. Rick's mother was fortunate to be hired as the secretary to the museum's director and, on the side, as a manuscript typist for well known historian, Ralph Nading Hill, who also served on the museum's board of directors. She was a hard worker, often typing late into the night for Mr. Hill, her fingers and wrists sore from producing seven carbon copies at a time on a manual typewriter for one cent a page.

As part of his mother's compensation package, Rick's family was able to live at the museum in an apartment over the toy shop. Rick told me that beneath his bedroom was a display area that housed two extremely rare, white porcelain swans, made in the 1750's in Chelsea, England. At that time they were each valued at over $200,000. They are now considered priceless. Needless to say, Rick remembered his mother being more than a little nervous about him getting into mischief and breaking the precious swans or other valuable artifacts. Therefore, she strictly forbade him to be home unless she was there to supervise him. As she worked very long hours on a regular basis, much of the time Rick had to find ways to entertain himself out of the house. Luckily, his playground included the expansive grounds of the museum as well as the bucolic surrounding countryside. One of the groundskeeper's sons became Rick's friend, and for several years they regularly fished together, riding their bikes to neighboring streams and ponds as well as down to the shores of Lake Champlain. As a young boy, Rick was most comfortable when he was away from the house, exploring the outdoors.

Rick often interacted with Mrs. Webb, who was very kind to him as he was part of the museum family. She enjoyed showing Rick unusual or amusing artifacts from her collection, pieces she didn't necessarily show to others, including a hand-painted, porcelain toilet pot hidden under the seat of an ornate 19th Century stagecoach. Occasionally Mrs. Webb's famous friends visited the museum, including Hollywood actress, Zasu Pitts, who Rick remembered arriving at the museum, chauffeured in her gleaming Rolls Royce. Rick was home when Mrs. Webb brought the actress over to his building to show her the famous swans, and he appreciated that Mrs. Webb took the time to personally introduce him to Ms. Pitts.

Rick recalled those days with a smile, "Mrs. Webb was very nice to me but sometimes I think I became a bit too much for her, so she'd quietly give me a dollar (a huge amount for a kid in those days) to deliver a string of sleigh bells or some other trinket to a distant corner of the property just to get rid of me. But she always treated me with respect and with things often pretty icy at home, that felt good."

Rick's mother was always worried about him getting into mischief, so the summer after they moved to the museum, in 1952, his maternal grandmother paid for him to be sent off to Camp Abnaki, a boys' camp in the Lake Champlain Islands. Rick recalled that time, "Back then it seemed like a long trip from Shelburne to the camp in North Hero. The sand bar from the mainland had a very narrow road with white painted boulders on the edges and every time you went, you drove around turtles slowly walking back and forth across the road. I remember that first year, as ironically I got terminally homesick and only lasted a couple of weeks before whining my way back home, much to my mother's displeasure. A couple of days after I fled the camp, a case of polio was discovered and the whole place was quarantined for a period of weeks. I later heard everybody had to get shots every day, so I *just* missed that delight."

Despite not lasting long, Rick had enjoyed the Abnaki atmosphere with camaraderie, campfires and lots of s'mores, and agreed to go back the next summer. He ended up having a great time and continued to attend the ten week summer sessions for the next five years. "In addition to the usual camp life in the cabins, as well as swimming and fishing and shooting archery, we also went on week long canoe trips around northern Lake Champlain in long Old Town canoes that carried six kids and a counselor. We paddled way up the Richelieu River into Quebec and camped out at the 1819 Fort Lennox, as well as at Fort Blunder at Rouse's Point, New York. We even canoed up the Ausable River to the famous Ausable Chasm. On another trip, we camped for a week in primitive Long Trail cabins up near the alpine zone on Mount Mansfield. We also took annual summer trips to Montreal to ride the open-air trolleys that are now long gone. It's hard to believe that Camp Abnaki hauled us kids around, 30 at a time, sitting on hay bales in the back of an old stake-body truck."

During evenings at Camp Abnaki the boys watched movies in the dining hall and that was when Rick saw his first Gene Autry movie. Another year they were shown the serial, *Phantom Empire*, which was a favorite that lasted all summer. Rick especially enjoyed what he described as "a very cool folk singer," who came up from New York City to lead the campers in singing traditional songs around the campfire. His summers at Abnaki turned out to be special times out in nature that made a lasting positive impression.

Back at the museum, one of the greatest events of Rick's boyhood, perhaps of his life, occurred on a cold day in November of 1954, when Mrs. Webb had the great Lake Champlain steamboat, *Ticonderoga* moved overland from Shelburne Harbor to the museum. Built and launched at Shelburne Shipyard in 1906, the *Ti* carried immense historical significance as it was not only the last steamer ever built and operated on Lake Champlain, it was in fact the last American side-paddle-wheel steamer in existence, designated a National Historic Landmark in 1964.

The *Ticonderoga's* storied history includes working for many years as a passenger and freight boat making regular runs between different ports in New York and Vermont. It was also called upon for ceremonial excursions, including in 1909 for the Tercentennial of Samuel de Champlain's discovery of Lake Champlain. During that grand celebration, the patriotically decorated *Ti* carried an impressive group of dignitaries including President William Taft, the ambassadors of France and Great Britain, as well as the governors of Vermont and New York. The *Ti* was also rumored to have been used during Prohibition as a ferry for cars loaded with bootlegged liquor that had successfully eluded G-men when coming down out of Canada. Though such use was not condoned by its owners, it was reported that some deckhands went home with a bottle or two in their pockets, rewards for not turning in the smugglers.

In the 1930's, when the railroads took away much of its business, the owners of the *Ti*, Champlain Transportation Company, could no longer support its continued operation solely as a means of transportation. Thus, in 1937 they sold the Company to Vermont businessman Horace Corbin, who transformed the *Ticonderoga* into an elegant showboat complete with a full bar, dance hall, and slot machines. He even mounted a huge sign on the upper deck that read "Showboat" in giant neon letters. On weekends, famed Vermont big band leader Sterling Weed and his Imperial Orchestra conducted popular dance excursions out of St. Albans Bay as the *Ti* plied the waters along the Vermont shoreline.

Occasionally on Sundays, hundreds of soldiers from Fort Ethan Allen would ride a street trolley to the King Street Dock to spend a relaxing afternoon on the lake. Vermont was under strict *blue laws* that forbid the sale of liquor on the Lord's Day, so the captain of the *Ti* would leave Burlington Harbor and steam across the border into New York waters where the crew would break out a bountiful supply of liquor, making for some happy Sunday afternoons on the lake. The new showboat was enjoyed by many around the Champlain Valley but not by the local Coast Guard officers stationed in Burlington. They deemed the neon signs were so bright they endangered nighttime navigation and ordered Corbin to remove them.

Despite these efforts, by 1950, then owner Martin Fisher, to his dismay, knew there was no way to keep the *Ti* afloat financially so he decided to scrap the boat to get some of his money back. Not wanting to lose the *Ti*, historian Ralph Nading Hill initiated a spirited fund-raising campaign to save the boat and keep her operating on the lake. However, even with widespread public support it was clear no one would be able to keep the aging side-wheeler operating commercially. Hill then turned to his good friend Mrs. Webb for help, suggesting she purchase the *Ti* and make it part of her growing collection at the museum.

Mrs. Webb liked the idea and soon bought the boat thinking she'd turn it into an off-site, floating exhibit at Shelburne Harbor, a couple miles from the main museum. The logistics of that plan turned out to be too complicated, so she made the surprising decision to move the *Ti* to a permanent berth at the museum. Many locals thought she was crazy to attempt moving a boat that size, a feat they were not aware had ever been done. Mrs. Webb, however, was determined to make it work and already had a wealth of experience moving whole buildings to the museum, including a lighthouse, a schoolhouse and a stagecoach inn. How hard could moving a 220 foot steamboat be?

Rick shared with me the tremendous excitement surrounding the monumental task of moving the grand, steam-powered vessel. As Mrs. Webb later said, it took a "truly gigantic" engineering feat to move the 892 ton boat across two miles of frozen farmers' fields to its new home. This was also a good time for Rick's family, as his father returned to Shelburne that fall to try to reunite with Rick's mom. In was good timing as the museum staff, including Rick's family, was invited to ride with Mrs. Webb and other dignitaries on the *Ticonderoga* for her last ceremonial voyage to the south end of Shelburne Bay.

The *Ticonderoga* was then floated into a gigantic basin that excavators had dug adjacent to the south end of the lake. The basin was closed in and the *Ti* winched into position on heavy wooden cradles which were mounted on a custom laid, double railroad track which served as the launching point for the boat's overland journey to the museum. Once the water was pumped back into the lake, a determined and ingenious crew of engineers and skilled laborers worked tirelessly to advance the *Ti* in the direction of the museum at a rate of about 250 feet a day. Early on, crews fought the brutal winds and frigid cold of the Vermont winter as hundreds of people stopped to watch the strange but wonderful sight of the *Ti* moving slowly across the pastoral landscape.

Everyone knew they had to get the *Ti* to the museum before the ground thawed in the spring. Unfortunately, warm southern winds arrived unexpectedly in March, threatening to collapse the temporary railroad upon which the *Ti* rode. The project almost ran aground – literally – in the middle of a hayfield on the farm of Mr. Wentworth Bicknell. As the hard winter frost began to soften, the exhausted crews worked around the clock to keep the *Ti* moving, finally arriving at the museum 65 days after leaving Shelburne Harbor.

In a well known archive photograph of the *Ti* beginning its journey from the lake to its final home, Rick's family is seen standing together at the bow's railing. It is the only picture Rick ever saw of his whole family together. He remembered that time as extremely exciting though bitter sweet. Despite trying to reconcile, the event marked the end of his parents' marriage, but was also the dawning of a lifelong appreciation and love of Lake Champlain steamboats.

Rick shared with me that one of his major challenges during this time was a debilitating medical condition called *atopic dermatitis*, characterized by a nasty rash that affected much of his body. Though it was difficult for him to talk about, I appreciated his candor in reflecting back on it. "When the rash was active, every fold of my skin would break out, blister and bleed, and the itching and pain became so bad I couldn't sleep. Sometimes I would scratch my scalp till it was raw. It was brutal, particularly as people would just stare at my raw skin. It sure didn't make me feel very good and the result was I didn't want to be around people and I surely couldn't interact with girls very well. It was very socially isolating and I ended up alone and unhappy a lot of the time."

Rick's mother took him to a local dermatologist, who tried to figure out what he was allergic to by scratching his back with hundreds of needles containing what Rick called "venoms." His was a puzzling case as some weeks he'd be allergic to certain things and other weeks it would be something entirely different. Unfortunately, one of the constant allergens was wool, which in the 1950's was hard to avoid for a kid living in northern Vermont as most winter clothing was made of it.

Living in misery and with the specialists unable to pinpoint his exact allergies, Rick was treated with frequent oatmeal baths and pain medication and at one point was put on a strict, six-month diet consisting only of boiled white rice, lamb and apricot juice. Still unable to give him sufficient relief, Rick's doctors finally prescribed high dose cortisone tablets, which he stayed on for many months. The steroids helped calm the terrible dermatitis but caused him to start developing premature cataracts, which eventually compromised his vision.

When Rick was able, he worked for a local fellow, John Tracy, who grew a large vegetable garden just west of the museum. Tracy, whose family was among the original settlers of Shelburne, was an eccentric man. He was known for writing agricultural papers for the University of Vermont, as well as for randomly showing up at Rick's nearby elementary school, walking into his classroom and playing a couple of tunes on the piano. One summer Rick spent many hours laboring in Tracy's fields working off the cost of a new pair of glasses. Despite his mother's admonitions, Rick was balancing on top of the log fence that surrounded the museum, lost his balance and fell on his face. His mother was *not* happy and made him pay for the cost of the replacements working for Tracy for ten cents an hour. Rick also had a paper route for the *Burlington Free Press*, delivering 37 papers to homes along Route Seven every morning before school.

Rick's humorous wisecracking was a trait that mostly served him well over the years, though there were some older kids in town who didn't seem to appreciate his humor. One fellow in particular was a nasty bully, whom Rick recalled with a frown. "The kid was the son of the town constable and took great delight in beating me up whenever he caught sight of me during those early grade school years. It was a good day when he missed finding me so he couldn't beat the tar out of me."

Around the time of the great *Ti* move, Rick managed to get his sea legs under him enough that he decided it was time to teach his "chief bully" a good lesson. Looking back, he remembered the events of that day as one of his "greatest triumphs."

"It happened to be the year of the Jules Verne movie, *20,000 Leagues Under the Sea*, and my friend Jimmy and I had saved our cereal box tops and sent away for this cardboard periscope that we put to good use on the grounds of the museum." Rick chuckled as he recalled that wonderful afternoon. "Near where we lived over the toy shop was an exhibit called the Shaker Shed. Under the shed there was this old yellow 1850's water wagon, which was basically a very large wooden barrel mounted on wagon wheels. After school, Jimmy and I would crawl into that wagon and use it as our clubhouse. One of our favorite things to do was fill our pockets with apples, get into the wagon and wait for tourists to walk by. We'd slide our cardboard periscope up through the opening in the top of the wagon and when we'd spot a tourist within range we'd peg apples toward them, at least close enough to give them pause. It was a lot of fun because most of them never knew where the apples came from."

Rick considered himself a lucky kid to get to play inside the museum and to use the old water wagon as a clubhouse. It wasn't long before the bully got wind of the boys "serving" the tourists apples, and he told Rick he wanted in on the fun. Rick decided this was the chance he'd been waiting for to get even. "I told him that I wouldn't let him in the wagon with us unless he smoked this special pipe I was going to make for him as a sort of initiation ceremony."

To prepare for the bully's initiation and to avoid detection by his mother, one night Rick quietly snuck downstairs from their apartment and tip-toed past the porcelain swans into the General Store section of the building where he knew there were some 18th Century powder horns hanging from the overhead wooden beams. He climbed up and took down a couple of powder horns, shook them, and to his delight found they still had a fair amount of black powder inside. Next he snagged an antique clay pipe out of a storeroom and carefully filled it with the powder, which he affectionately referred to as "radioactive pepper," knowing how hot black powder burned. Following in his father's pyrotechnic footsteps, Rick prepared to pull off his prank.

Almost 60 years later, Rick still got excited when he talked about that afternoon. "That kid got all wound up when I told him we were going to let him into our secret club house. After school that day, he met us at the wagon and we all piled in through the square hatch, making him go first so he had to crawl into the way back, followed by Jimmy, his older brother Bill, and me. Before the ceremony began, I made sure everyone but the bully was close to the escape hatch and I checked outside to make sure there weren't any tourists around. I pulled out the old pipe, and the bully proudly put it in his mouth. I handed him a couple of those big wooden kitchen matches and he quickly lit the pipe, which was followed by a loud whooshing sound and an unbelievable amount of pure white smoke which instantly filled the wagon. Suddenly, we heard the big bully yelling "MAMA!!" at the top of his lungs, and I beat it out through the hatch with Jimmy and Bill hot on my tail."

When Rick hit the ground, he paused. "As long as I live, I will never forget what I saw looking back after I jumped off that big wagon wheel. That wagon was just a big long barrel on wheels and the wood was dry as a bone so there were spaces between the slats of the barrel. And just like someone was blowing perfect smoke rings, every opening had squirted a puff of white smoke into the air surrounding the wagon and it was just hanging there. My mind clicked a picture and then I ran like hell. Probably the first *photograph* I ever took."

Rick said the bully came screaming out of the wagon last, taking off across the museum grounds like a jack rabbit. That night, his father called Rick's mother and told her that Rick had burned his son's eyebrows and some of his hair off in addition to scaring the bejesus out of him. Worried he would once again be in trouble with his mother, Rick was relieved and happy when she told the bully's father that it served the kid right for beating Rick up all the time. Mercifully, that was the end of it.

In an effort to keep Rick out of mischief, his mother arranged for him to take formal guitar lessons from a fellow named, Leonard Knight, who attempted to teach Rick how to read sheet music and play by memorizing each individual note. Rick tried to learn, but Knight's method did not come naturally. Rick paid for the lessons by working Saturdays in Knight's body shop in his barn, sanding repaired panels on Chevrolet sedans by hand. After a few months, Rick had had enough of both the sanding and the formal guitar lessons and was able to back out of them. If that was what playing a musical instrument was going to be like, it was no fun and Rick wanted nothing to do with it.

During those difficult grade school years, Rick became friends with the Sinnott family, particularly with their sons, Jimmy, Bill and Larry, who were "older and cooler" than Rick. They originally lived on a farm in the village where the museum's double covered bridge now stands, but back in the early 1950's, Mrs. Webb had purchased their land and moved their farmhouse and chicken coop to the south end of town. "Larry was my hero as a kid. He treated me with respect, and his family let me spend a lot of time with them, which was very special to me with my mother working so much and the way things were at home." Larry also interested Rick in listening to music on the radio and on records, especially songs from Louis "Satchmo" Armstrong, and other jazz musicians. This new pastime seemed to awaken something in Rick and gave him a way to escape – at least for a short while – from the stressful parts of his life.

Poignantly, the first record Rick ever bought was Elvis' 1956 megahit, "Love Me Tender." That summer Rick saved up enough money and bought the single at Bailey's Music Rooms in downtown Burlington and, record in hand, ran up to the YMCA and proudly showed it to some friends.

When Rick was in fifth grade, Larry enlisted in the Marine Corps and left Vermont for training. When he returned, he got a bunch of the neighborhood kids together and formed the "Junior Marine Club." The club looked very official as the boys had uniforms and regularly held meetings and *basic training* in the Sinnott family's chicken coop, which served as their headquarters. Larry was into the military way of life and taught his young recruits the Marine's General Orders, which they could recite from memory, as well as other basic skills, including how to field strip an M-I riffle. Occasionally, Larry arranged to take his club down to the Naval Reserve Building on the Burlington waterfront, where they hung out with some of the local officers. Rick described himself as "an avid participant" until some Marine brass got wind of what was going on and made the club disband as they were impersonating United States military personnel.

As a young teenager, Rick's interest in music deepened and he spent more time listening to and singing along with songs on the radio. He remembered "Hang Down Your Head Tom Dooley" was one of his favorites. "It sounds kind of strange to think of it in those terms, but I spent most of my time as a young kid trying to survive. I just didn't have much direction in my life until I got interested in music and saw that as a vehicle for making something good happen. Music, particularly when it involved other people, started to become something positive I could really focus on."

Rick once again became interested in playing an instrument and during one of his occasional visits to Shelburne, his father brought him a five string banjo. As Rick had considered his previous attempt at formal music instruction "boring and limiting," he started playing around on the banjo himself, learning to play a little by ear. That was the beginning of what would become a lifelong love of music, both as an admirer and as a performer.

Another blessing in Rick's early life was his eighth grade teacher, Becky Blanchard, who took him under her wing. She recalled, "From the first day I met him, Ricky had a special light in his eyes as well as an irresistible, mischievous smile. And he was the brightest kid in my class, always genuinely curious about people and looking for the good in everyone."

Rick often stayed after school in Becky's classroom, most often because he'd gotten into trouble, but sometimes because he had nowhere else to go. At the time, Becky was being courted by a fellow named Rene who would stop by the school after work to see her. Before long, Rick and Rene became friends and started playing chess together while Becky corrected papers. She looked back, "I think things were real tough for Ricky at home around the time his mom got divorced and then took up with another roughneck guy who worked at the museum snack bar. I think that Ricky felt safe with us, and we sure loved having him around, so my husband and I sort of adopted him."

Becky smiled, and then added, "I must tell you Ricky was also a little prankster and on more than one occasion got my class in a bit of trouble when we would go over to visit the Shelburne Museum on a field trip. Living at the museum, Ricky basically had the run of the place and would somehow talk us into doing things that were not quite allowed by the museum's rules. Like the day he convinced us all to sneak downstairs onto one of the big, off-limits display floors which housed Mrs. Webb's collection of vintage wagons. That rascal got the whole class, including me, to climb all over those beautiful antique wagons which, of course, was strictly forbidden. We had a great time pretending we were on a westward wagon train until a museum guide showed up and ordered us to get off the fragile wagons. Ricky thought it was great fun – especially the getting us in trouble part. And I have to admit, I did too."

Rick told me how supportive the Blanchards were and that he has enjoyed keeping in touch with them ever since. "As far as my family went, if you looked up the definition of 'dysfunctional family' you'd probably find a picture of us. I had to work out most of how to do life by myself, but Becky and her husband helped me out a lot. They were so kind to me, and at that point I really needed that."

Another exciting Shelburne escapade involved Rick and a cap-and-ball musket he bought for five dollars from Wally White's gun shop at the back of The Harbor Hideaway, a local restaurant. Having seen they used a sawed-off rifle on the TV western, *Wanted Dead or Alive*, Rick decided to put his musket to good use by sawing it off and convincing one of his friends to try and actually fire it. Inside their family's garage at the museum, Rick filled the shortened musket with smokeless powder, which burns even hotter than traditional black powder. When his buddy pulled the trigger, the barrel exploded and shot through the roof of the garage. His friend started screaming and took off through the garage doors, followed by Rick, who didn't want to be associated with the damage. Luckily, no one got seriously hurt and no one – particularly his mother – connected him with the hole in the roof.

Despite the demise of that old musket, through living at the Museum, Rick developed an appreciation for the value of history, antiques and fine craftsmanship of many kinds. Mrs. Webb's wonderful "collection of collections" represented something solid in his life – beautiful, functional things that taught him about the importance of the past.

By the time Rick turned 15, his mother married that short order cook who worked at the museum's snack bar and had once worked as a deck hand on the *Ti*. Rick shared with me that his new stepfather had a serious drinking problem, which made Rick's home situation much worse. By the end of his sophomore year in high school, he knew his Shelburne days had to come to an end. "I had extreme unhappiness with the stepfather situation as he was physically abusive when drunk and he was drunk a lot. I recall one time in particular having to ride with my mother while she trolled through the dingy bars on North Street in Burlington trying to find him during a many-day drunk. I was very upset as I had high school exams the next day and was instead involved in looking for a mean drunk. Back in those days there were a lot of ugly scenes for sure."

If Rick was to actually thrive and not just survive in the world, he knew he had to make a big change. Soon he would meet the greatest mentor of his life, a special man who was involved in traditional music on several levels. He was also a man who revered the intriguing history of Vermont.

Chapter Three

BACK TO HARDWICK

By the spring of 1961, at age 16, Rick needed to make a plan to leave Shelburne. His father was being discharged from the Army after 25 years of service and had decided to use the GI Bill to attend a hotel management school in Washington, DC, that fall. He was unable to bring Rick with him to school but agreed to take custody and moved Rick to live with his grandmother in East Hardwick. Then his father drove them all to Houlton, Maine, where they spent a couple of weeks visiting relatives, after which they returned to his Grandmother Delilah's house in East Hardwick, where his dad spent the rest of the summer. It was a summer that Rick remembered well, as his dad bought an aluminum boat with a trolling motor and they enjoyed a fair amount of time together fishing on nearby Caspian Lake. Rick's dad also taught him how to drive that summer. It was the most quality time he had ever spent with his father, and also, the last.

Living back in East Hardwick, Rick was immersed in the company of his grandmother's contemporaries, many of whom were in their seventies. Having spent her entire career as a nurse caring for the people of the town, she was beloved by the community and her group of friends made Rick feel right at home. He particularly enjoyed hearing the old timers tell stories about traditional rural Vermont and later said that those encounters were influential on his eventual songwriting career. Rick also enjoyed being able to chum around with his cousins from the Eastman side of the family with whom he'd kept in touch over the years during weekend visits and summer vacations.

Living with his grandmother was at times, however, an entirely different matter. Rick remembered it this way. "When I came to live with Grammy Dell, she was 78 years old and had recently gotten out of the hospital after recovering from a diabetic coma that nearly killed her. She was in really rough shape and sometimes acted very strangely. Shortly after I moved in she accused her prominent neighbor, Jack Hancock, the Speaker of the Vermont House, of sneaking in and stealing her portable washing machine from her kitchen. Of course that was utter nonsense, but she wouldn't let it go as once she set her mind to something, there was no changing it." Rick shook his head and continued. "I never knew what Grammy was going to do next; like the time she hid her purse in her freezer for six weeks, while obsessively looking all over the place for it. On the other hand, I was glad to be living back in East Hardwick and grateful that the old gal got me up in the morning, cooked me breakfast and treated me like family. It was a damn sight better than the drunken abuse I put up with in Shelburne."

Rick soon connected with his grandmother's next door neighbor, a warm-hearted Renaissance man named, Harold Patch. A Jack London-esq man, Patch and his wife had retired to East Hardwick a few years before and were living a largely self-sustaining life. As a young man, Patch served in the Army in World War I and later became a well known radio personality who played live music in the mid 1930's on WDEV in Waterbury, Vermont, where he also worked as a machinist. Mr. Patch was a prolific gardener, journalist and a talented folk musician.

The Patches led an intellectually stimulating life and put great value on reading and music. Two of the Patch's children were born blind and they had attended the renowned Perkins School for the Blind in Boston, where they were taught Braille and other skills so that they could live as independently as possible. Some of the family's favorite books were written by Vermont author and folklorist, Rowland E. Robinson, who lived on a farm named Rokeby, in the town of Ferrisburg on the western side of the State. A family of devout Quakers, the Robinsons were staunch abolitionists deeply involved in the *Underground Railroad*, their farm considered to be one of the best documented *stations* of the 1830's and 1840's. During that time his parents harbored many fugitive slaves, helping them escape to Canada out of the reach of dreaded southern slave catchers. Rokeby is now a museum and National Historic Landmark.

Like so many others, the Patches endured hard times after the Depression in the early 1930's. Work was limited in Vermont but Mr. Patch read that there were good jobs available in Florida. Taking a chance they could make a better living in *The Land of Opportunity*, he converted their Model T Ford into a primitive camper, loaded the family into it and headed south. It was a long, difficult journey to the Sunshine State and they soon found out that those plentiful jobs didn't exist. Realizing their trip was a boondoggle and their money running low, they headed back to Vermont as fast as they could.

Back in Vermont, Mr. Patch was able to get a job in Springfield working as a machinist for Jones and Lampson Company. He also scraped together enough money to buy a small farm in the central Vermont hamlet of Perkinsville, along the banks of the Branch Brook, where the Patches raised food for their family for many years. Eventually, the government decided to build a dam on a nearby river that would have permanently flooded all of their productive fields. Not having the energy to fight a battle they knew they couldn't win, the Patches sold out to the government and retired to East Hardwick.

The Patches came north with as many possessions as they could carry, including a farm truck loaded with barrels of corn, flour, and maple syrup he had stockpiled for their retirement. Once established in their new home, they continued to grind their own cornmeal and make their own bread, donuts and other baked goods. They heated with wood and cultivated a large vegetable garden that, with the help of lots of canning, provided them with homegrown produce year round.

During our many discussions, there was a reverence in Rick's voice as he told me about his special friendship with Harold Patch. "My life changed dramatically when I started hanging out with Mr. Patch. He was wicked nice to me, and I really looked up to him for all the different things he knew how to do and did well. He influenced me greatly in my lifelong career choices and interests, including music, journalism, and photography. As a man, I honestly think I learned everything I ever needed to know from Mr. Patch. It was from him that I got most of my instruction on life, including reinforcement of the importance of a strong work ethic, which I'd had a taste of working in John Tracy's garden in Shelburne. Mr. Patch also taught me how much fun it was to play music with other people and the importance and value of learning and preserving local history."

Harold Patch was an avid history buff whose father, William Patch, was born in 1846 in a primitive log cabin in Morristown, Vermont. William served with the Vermont regiments in the Union Army during the Civil War and, according to family history, helped build the fortifications around Washington, DC, which defended against the Confederate Army approaching from the south. Harold's daughter, Lorraine, remembers, "My grandfather, William, told my father that one day President Lincoln came out from the White House to see how the fortification work was progressing and stood within sight of the Confederates with his foot on the embankment built to protect the city. A shot was fired at the Union Army that narrowly missed President Lincoln, who never winced and said, "You'll have to be a better shot than that." William fought gallantly in and survived several battles including, it is believed, the legendary Battle of Cedar Creek, which took a staggering toll on the Union Army and the Vermont Regiments in particular.

Harold Patch was keenly interested in preserving his own family's history as well as that of his home state. In 1954 he was one of the co-founders of the

Vermont "251 Club," a group of Green Mountain enthusiasts dedicated to learning about and visiting all 251 of Vermont's towns. His family camped almost every weekend in their 1949 Chevy station wagon he had modified into a camper by fashioning a rack on the roof that held a mattress and installing a wood cook stove in the back of the car, the centerpiece of their mobile kitchen. Rick told me Mr. Patch "was a man of seemingly boundless energy who did more in a day than most people could even *think* of doing."

Harold Patch made what little money he could as a correspondent and photographer for the *Hardwick Gazette*, the *Burlington Free Press* and other newspapers that paid him a few pennies a line for his articles. Over the years, he wrote many entertaining stories about his young friend and protégé, Rick Norcross, including the night he could have easily frozen to death on the mountains of Smuggler's Notch.

Patch was also an active member of the Hardwick United Church and was good friends with the minister, who had a sweet tooth for maple syrup. Rick remembered times when Mr. Patch, a twinkle in his eye, would bring out a special batch of syrup he had brought with him when he retired to East Hardwick. While that particular syrup had a rich maple flavor to it, it also seemed to have a powerful, intestinal gas-producing effect. When the good reverend partook of the liquid gold — especially when combined with Patch's homemade raised donuts — the reverend would soon commence passing large amounts of uncontrollable and quite audible wind, which Patch found extremely funny. However, even that rather shocking result didn't dampen the reverend's appetite for Mr. Patch's special syrup. He always asked for a refill.

One day in Mr. Patch's kitchen, he showed Rick an old fiddle and a guitar. Patch told him he hadn't played in years but that he'd like to get back to fiddling and that Rick "would be doing him a favor if he'd learn the guitar," so that Patch would have someone to play with. Rick loved listening to Mr. Patch's renditions of the old songs and quickly took him up on his offer. Mr. Patch had a very folksy style and was able to teach Rick how to play chords, strum and pick the guitar by ear, which seemed a much more natural way of learning than the unsuccessful formal lessons Rick had struggled with and abandoned in Shelburne.

Rick took to the guitar with great interest and was soon practicing several hours a day, which kept him out from under his grandmother's feet. Observing that Rick had a keen sense of humor and a proclivity for telling good stories, Mr. Patch encouraged him to start writing his own songs. He also sold Rick his first guitar, letting him work off the $30 price stacking firewood and weeding in his vegetable garden. Rick's gratitude for his grandmother's neighbor ran deep. "Harold Patch was my greatest mentor and hero. He had such a hugely positive influence on me, and I've tried to take a lot of him with me throughout my life. I loved him like a grandfather and will always be so grateful he was in my life."

Encouraged by local ministers, Rick soon began playing music with area church groups, which reminded him of the special experiences he'd had around the campfires at Camp Abnaki. "Between Mr. Patch and Reverend John Nutting, I got all fired up about singing and playing in front of people in their church's youth groups. It was such a warm atmosphere and seeing what a musical instrument could do for a group of people fascinated me. If someone liked your music, they opened their heart to you and that was so exciting for me — like I'd stepped into a whole new world."

Growing up in Shelburne, Rick had been a loner much of the time, but in East Hardwick he discovered a more normal social life where he was able to connect with his cousins and make new friends through playing music together. Life there, however, still had its challenges, particularly as the winters were brutally cold with nighttime temperatures often dropping to more than thirty below zero. "Maybe the worst part of being back in East Hardwick was that my grandmother had no car, so unless I could hitch a ride I had to walk everywhere and it was four miles from our house to school over in Hardwick. I was often out in the evening practicing or performing with my guitar, and back in those days there were very few cars on the road, particularly after dark. I still remember heading home bundled up in many layers and the crunching sound of ice and snow under my boots as I'd walk along the side of the road."

Sometimes Rick lucked out and hitched a ride with someone heading his way. The most memorable ride he got was with a fellow named Bud Boydston, who pulled over and picked him up one especially snowy evening in December of 1961. It turned out Boydston had recently moved to nearby Walden from Buena Park, California, where he was master of ceremonies for the entertainment at Knott's Berry Farm, a major tourist attraction. Having had enough of California craziness, Bud had bought a farm in Walden, sight unseen through the mail, and moved his family across the country to Vermont in a big 1949 Chrysler pulling a trailer full of their belongings.

Rick soon became part of the Boydston's extended family, spending weeks helping out on their farm during planting, haying and harvesting seasons. Though the long sweaty hours working in hot fields were bad for Rick's dermatitis, it was worth it to be around Bud's welcoming family, in part because Bud loved to play music, particularly in their farmhouse kitchen after dinner. Rick felt at home playing along with Bud, who was able to teach Rick many new songs. He looked back fondly on those days. "Bud really became another father figure for me, a very important member of my growing adopted family. He also had a big influence on me musically, and I was lucky enough to later perform with him professionally."

That first winter back in East Hardwick was full of adventures for the 17-year-old Norcross, who from a young age, always enjoyed being in the out-of-doors. None of his adventures, however, were more harrowing than that of January 11, 1962, when he nearly spent the night on frigid Sterling Mountain at the Jeffersonville ski area, which later became the Smugglers Notch Resort.

Rick got a ride to the ski area with a Hardwick Academy teacher, whose wife agreed to pick Rick up after a day on the mountain. Rick wasn't a skier but he was a skilled "jack jumper" rider, which was a handmade device with a wooden seat mounted by a short post to a single wooden ski. Riders would hang onto the seat while balancing with their feet to stay upright and steer. The Jeffersonville side of the mountains only had a Poma lift, which Rick could not ride with his jumper. So he put the jumper over his shoulder and trekked up Sterling Mountain in order to ride a trail down the Spruce Peak side into the Stowe ski area, which had a chairlift he could ride for the day. It took several hours to make it over the mountain. In an article written about the escapade by Mr. Patch for the *Burlington Free Press,* Rick said his long hike up and over Sterling Pond "was not all pleasure as I dropped into the deep snow clear to my hips more than once!"

Rick rode down a Spruce Peak trail, then crossed the Notch Road and caught a ride on the single chairlift to the top of Mount Mansfield, Vermont's highest peak. After taking an exhilarating ride down the long Toll Road, the afternoon was waning, so Rick started heading back to meet his ride home. He walked across to the Spruce Peak base area to ride the chairlift up the mountain to return to the Jeffersonville side. When he got to the chairlift, he found it had just closed for the day. This left Rick in a quandary. He knew there were folks on the Stowe side who could give him a ride home to Hardwick, but felt he "couldn't very well leave his friends waiting for him on the Jeffersonville side in a lurch." He decided to make the long trek back up Spruce Peak on foot, again carrying his trusty jack jumper over his shoulder.

When Rick reached the ski patrol hut at the top of Spruce Peak, the sun had set on the other side of the mountain and the temperature was rapidly falling. He was sweaty and cold and decided to go inside the hut to try and warm up before heading another mile across frozen Sterling Pond to the Jeffersonville side of the mountains. Fortunately, there were still hot coals in the woodstove, and after awhile he warmed himself enough to get ready for what he hoped would be the final leg of his long day in the snow. For most people the thought of crossing a mountain range after dark in the middle of winter would seem too threatening to consider, but for Rick it just seemed the thing to do. Perhaps that strength came from the camping he did through Camp Abnaki, where he once spent a week in the alpine zone on top of Mt. Mansfield. As was often the case in his life, he was comfortable out trekking alone, relying on his faith the natural world would somehow carry him along.

By the time Rick had hiked across the frozen pond to the summit of Sterling Mountain, the moon illuminated the trails enough for him to navigate his way down to the ski area parking lot. His jack jumper was challenging enough to ride in broad daylight, so Rick had to hold on especially tight as he rocketed down the icy mountainside. As he neared the bottom of the nearly 2000 foot drop, he could see automobile lights in the parking lot below him. Excited, he raced toward the bottom, failing to recognize a good sized mogul that had built up in the middle of the trail. Suddenly catapulted through the air, Rick landed with such force the hardwood seat of the jack jumper split in two, and he continued to career down the slick trail on his bruised "keester."

When Rick righted himself there appeared to be only one car left in the parking lot, and it was making its way to the exit. Not to be deterred, he gathered up his broken jack jumper and ran down the rest of the hill as fast as he could. But he wasn't able to catch that last car, and his spirits and body sagged.

Rick told me that by then he was cold to his core and totally exhausted. He knew he might well freeze to death if he didn't keep moving. "I have to admit I had kind of a funny feeling in my stomach when I saw those last tail lights go out of sight." Having no other alternative, Rick started walking – past the silent ski lifts, the darkened base lodge and parking lots – toward town. He kept rubbing his hands together to try to keep the feeling in his fingers, pushing himself as hard as he ever had to trudge the six more miles down a frozen road to Jeffersonville village. The colder it got, the slower he walked, but he finally made it and was greatly relieved to find the lights were still on in the general store. Inside, the shop keep kindly let him make a phone call to find a ride home. Remembering back to that fateful night, Rick recalled, "After it got dark and the temperature plummeted, I took comfort in telling myself

— over and over again — that I couldn't be in that much trouble 'cause I was in Vermont. Just knowing that I was in my home state gave me enough comfort to keep going. But I can tell you I was one happy fellow when my cousin, Charlie Cook, came and fetched me back to East Hardwick. I finally fell into my grandmother's toasty house about ten o'clock that night."

Though Rick was still a musical neophyte, during his junior year in high school his commitment to learning to play the guitar and banjo deepened. In the summer of 1962 he met a girl named Krissy at a church camp and through her became interested in contemporary folk musicians like Ramblin' Jack Elliot and Pete Seeger. Encouraged by Mr. Patch and the songs of Seeger and Woody Guthrie, Rick discovered what a gift it was to write original songs, particularly ones that spoke to important current events. One such tune with a strong social conscience dealt with the 1962 Cuban Missile Crisis, and after Rick finished it he got up the "gumption" to mail the lyrics to Pete Seeger.

To Rick's surprise and delight, he received a postcard back from Seeger saying he really liked the song. He even invited Rick to come to an annual benefit concert he gave at the Country School in Woodstock, Vermont, a progressive school that his son and daughter attended. When his friend Krissy heard of Seeger's invitation, she asked Rick to come down and stay with her family and they would go to the show together. Rick could scarcely believe his good fortune and was soon hitchhiking his way to Woodstock.

Krissy, her mom and Rick had excellent seats at the concert, and even got to meet Seeger before the show, which was a real thrill. Seeger's performance featured both traditional and protest folk songs and his signature singalongs. Then, in the middle of the show, Seeger suddenly turned to Rick and announced that this young Vermont fellow sitting in the audience had sent him the words to a good song that he had written. He asked Rick to come up on stage and sing it for them. Rick stayed in his seat mortified. Though he had written the words to the song, unbeknownst to Seeger, Rick was still trying to figure out how to play it and certainly wasn't ready to perform it in front of anyone. In addition, he was still learning how to play the guitar in general. As Rick told me with trepidation in his voice, "that moment began the worst ten minutes of my life."

Rick sheepishly stepped up onto the stage, and Seeger handed him his 12 string guitar, a rather complicated instrument Rick had never seen before, let alone played. Knowing there was no way he could perform the song, Rick looked over at Seeger standing at the side of the stage, waiting. As had been the case in many difficult situations in his life, Rick instinctively turned to his sense of humor to make it through the excruciatingly uncomfortable moment. "I tried to make light of the situation, like it was all a joke, but I made a complete fool of myself. I stood there unable to play, my cheeks and neck blushing fire red with embarrassment. And standing just a few feet away was one of my greatest musical heroes looking first confused then very angry with me. Seeger didn't get it that I was just a kid, that I could barely play a six string guitar let alone a twelve."

When Rick talked about that incident nearly 50 years later, it was still difficult for him. "I felt terrible and finally just slunk off the stage back to my seat, where Krissy and her Mom looked totally disgusted with me. I felt really badly about the whole thing, and I'm sure Seeger did, too. To this day, I'm still upset about it, particularly that Seeger must have thought I was being disrespectful or was making fun of the situation, which was not at all the case. Years later, when I was performing professionally, I saw Seeger backstage at Carnegie Hall, and he wouldn't speak to me. That was very painful."

Despite this crushing experience, by then Rick was developing a deepening interest in music and writing songs and he "just kept on going," something he had to do repeatedly in his life. Supported by a lot of positive feedback from new friends, by his late teens, a quick-witted, natural performer started to emerge from beneath the protective shell he had lived under for so long. Rick soon began playing at local venues including The Fortnightly Club, which was associated with the Hardwick United Church. He typically sang a short set of folk songs, featuring selections from Pete Seeger's *Broadside* album, including "Dr. Freud," and "The Wild West is Where I Want to Be."

Audiences enjoyed Rick's performances and that gave him some self-confidence. That was strongly reinforced one evening when a prominent local businessman named, Rod Montgomery, came up to Rick after a performance, patted him on the shoulder, and said, "That was a great show, kid. Keep at it and you're going to go somewhere."

Rick shared with me that at that point he had no real plan for the future, but it was perhaps the first time it occurred to him he might just amount to something. Since early childhood he had been living mostly on basic instinct, feeling responsible for his own survival – both physically and emotionally. With the discovery of wonderful and supportive people associated with music, Rick began coming into his own as a creative young man developing a talent for entertaining others.

Over the next year, Rick performed his own material at churches, summer camps, and eventually at larger Vermont venues like the *Vermont Dairy Days* festival in Enosburg Falls. He even entertained auction crowds for comedic Northeast Kingdom auctioneer, Albert May, known as "The Man with the Derby Hat." During breaks in the auction, Rick played a few folk songs while Mr. May rested. When he was ready to resume the bidding, May climbed back up on stage, thanked Rick for entertaining the crowd and threw him some random item, like a bundle of old dish towels tied together with twine. "Believe it or not," Rick recalled, "that was more than I got paid for a lot of gigs."

The response from audiences – particularly to his original material – was encouraging and though Rick couldn't quite see the path ahead, he realized music was going to be central to his life. He also felt a growing appreciation for the kind people who helped him along the way, including his English teacher at Hardwick Academy, Miss Joanne Schuler. Schuler was a longtime friend of fellow Austrian, the Baroness Maria Von Trapp and lived at the Trapp Family Lodge in Stowe, a popular and rapidly growing resort situated on an idyllic mountainside just south of the village. Miss Schuler commuted 25 miles each way from her home in Stowe to Hardwick so that she could teach at the Academy.

Like Rick's eighth grade teacher, Becky Blanchard, Miss Schuler saw something special in him and wanted to help him further his interest in music. She also knew that money was tight in his family and he was tired of farm work, so in the fall of 1962 she was able to get him a job working as a dishwasher at the Trapp Family Lodge in Stowe. Rick hitchhiked back and forth to work on weekends and stayed at Trapp's during school vacations. He appreciated what a great opportunity it was and worked very hard, gradually being promoted to waiter and wine steward in the upscale restaurant.

For Rick, working at Trapp's was like stepping into another world. He hitched over to Stowe, climbed out of his overalls and into the official Trapp outfit, which consisted of black pants, starched white shirt and a custom red vest bedecked with gleaming gold buttons. "We all looked pretty fancy and certainly dressed and acted the part. Sometimes guests would ask me if I was one of the Trapps, and I would smile and, in my best Austrian accent say: "Yeaas, yeaas, of course."

The following summer, one of Rick's responsibilities was cleaning the swimming pool and attending to the needs and fancies of the guests relaxing in the sun. "I can tell you that working at the Trapp Family Lodge was surely a better gig than slaving on a dusty farm in the hot sun all day. Here I was, working at this upscale resort surrounded with beautiful, bored 'Rolls Royce daughters' lounging around looking for someone to play with. Pretty heady stuff for a kid from East Hardwick."

Rick had vivid memories of the famed Baroness. "She ruled her mountainside kingdom with a stern hand, insisting that everyone who worked for her call her Mother. The Baroness was always dressed in her native Austrian *dirndl* and was the queen of the place. I was real grateful for the job but at times Mother could be a tyrant to work for. Everything was done her way, without discussion

– period. Growing up in my house, I knew what that was like. Truth is a lot of local people in Stowe were scared to death of her.

"On the other hand, the whole Trapp deal was a big economic boon for the town because at that time the *Sound of Music* was a huge musical on Broadway that was loosely based on her life story. Rich and important people from New York and other cities flocked to the Trapp Family Lodge just to be near the Baroness. Those of us who worked there also saw another, more mortal side of her. Most people didn't realize that during those years the Baroness suffered from recurrent bouts of malaria that she had acquired working at a mission school her family generously sponsored in the South Pacific islands. She would end up sick in bed, sometimes for a week at a time, and that certainly didn't help her disposition."

After Rick had been there for awhile, the Baroness realized he was something of a folk singer and asked him to perform for her guests. Rick knew it was a rare opportunity for him to reach a larger audience. "During one especially busy Christmas season, I guess the Baroness saw me dragging a guitar case around all the time so she allowed me to do a Wednesday night music session in the recreation room. Basically, the place was incredibly full so she welcomed another activity for the guests and took a chance and let me sing for them."

Rick played popular Pete Seeger and Woody Guthrie songs as well as a few original tunes and was glad to have a receptive audience. The Baroness must have been pleased as she asked him to continue his performances. Things actually went along quite well until one night when he was in the middle of a performance for an especially large audience. He was in the process of introducing a folk song by Woody Guthrie when the Baroness suddenly burst from the back of the room and strode down the aisle straight at Rick in her full *dirndl* regalia.

Mortified, Rick stopped speaking in mid-sentence. "She came right up to me, shaking her large finger in my face and told me in her booming voice: 'A

36

song is not a *folk* song if you know who wrote it. They are *only* passed down through tradition."

Seeing the fire in her eyes and realizing what a musical purist the Baroness must be, Rick was scared out of his wits and certainly wasn't going to argue with her. "Having been sternly corrected by the Baroness Maria Von Trapp during a performance in front of a hundred of her highbrow guests, I just shriveled up on the spot. It was yet another one of my magic moments on stage."

After Mother spun on her heel and stormed out of the room, Rick composed himself enough to go on. Before he began the Guthrie tune, he carefully enunciated to the audience, with just a pinch of sarcasm, "I just want to be clear that this next selection is *not* a folk song."

Fortunately, interactions with the Baroness weren't always that testy. In fact, she sometimes told Rick stories about the Trapp Family Singers' tours when they performed all over the United States and around the world. Ironically, one of their most memorable performances occurred at – of all places – the East Hardwick Congregational Church. It was 1949, the Trapps were an extremely popular group and the church, built in 1830, was packed literally wall-to-wall with people. The Baroness told Rick that right after performing their second song, there was a loud creaking noise and the wooden floor of the church started to collapse under the tremendous weight of the crowd. This left the church deeply bowed in the center.

In attendance that evening were several town fathers who helped evacuate the hundreds of people from the building, most of whom seemed more upset at missing the concert than the fact the church was collapsing beneath them. Sensing they might have a rebellion on their hands, the men decided to have a look under the church and see how badly it was damaged. Because there was no basement under the old structure, they determined that the floor probably wouldn't collapse any further, so to the delight of the crowd they let everyone back in where they sat in the sagging pews for the rest of the concert.

Usually at the end of their concerts the Baroness would bring the audience to their feet and lead them in a stirring rendition of the "Star Spangled Banner," but that night the town fathers forbid it for fear the force of the huge crowd suddenly standing in unison might cause the entire church to cave in. The Baroness was not happy about it, but understood. She told Rick that was the only time in all the years her family toured that the audience did not stand for her adopted country's national anthem and it still bothered her. Rick enjoyed performing at the Trapp Family Lodge and for a couple of years continued to appear there whenever he could.

During those two long winters attending Hardwick Academy, Rick often daydreamed during classes about living in a warmer climate. Sometimes he drifted away from the subject at hand entirely, drawing pictures of palm trees in his school notebooks while the snow blew hard against the rattling windows. He also continued to suffer with his dermatitis, which at times was so bad he had to go to Walter Reed Army Hospital for intensive treatments to get it under control. Despite whatever else was going on, Rick continued to practice his guitar six or more hours a day, and by his senior year was performing on a regular basis, including at a spring concert that was part of the annual *Hardwick Tulip Festival.*

Regardless of how much he enjoyed living in Vermont, by that time Rick Norcross was dreaming of bigger things – things he could do with his music outside the tiny Northeast Kingdom, and his feet were getting restless.

Chapter Four

ON A SOUTHBOUND TRAIN-I'M FROM VERMONT, I DO WHAT I WANT!

As much as he loved Vermont, Rick's burgeoning interest in music drew his attention to the world beyond the Green Mountains. He had enjoyed his two years in East Hardwick, but at age 18 decided to head south to get away from the ferocious winters and to avail himself of new musical opportunities. He applied to and was accepted at Florida Southern College (FSC), where he figured the weather would be more hospitable. Not that he hadn't had his share of fun during his time at Hardwick Academy, including the night he and his friends attended the junior prom, thoughtfully giving their dates formaldehyde-scented corsages from the cooler at Harold Holcomb's Funeral Home, the only place in town that sold fresh flowers.

In June of 1963, Rick took a train to Union Station in Washington, DC, which of course was built from solid Hardwick granite. From there he boarded a special private coach reserved for FSC freshman from the Northeast, and off they went down through the Blue Hills and horse ranches of Virginia, past the Smokey Mountains of the Carolinas, across Georgia and into the Sunshine State.

Rick had a great time on the ride south as the train was full of excited kids looking forward to their freshman year at college. Several of them had brought portable record players and Rick and a couple others had brought guitars, so the coach was filled with music, singing and all around good fun. As they finally passed through northern Florida on their way to Lakeland, Rick enjoyed the miles of colorful orange and grapefruit groves that stretched as far as the eye could see. He was surprised, however, at how incredibly flat the landscape was.

Once settled on the FSC campus, Rick was delighted to find many people in the area had a strong interest in folk music. He soon connected with other singers, though there seemed to be very few places in which to play. Hungry to start performing again, he discovered there was going to be a *Hootenanny Contest* at the Polk Theater in downtown Lakeland. Rick recalled that event with a mischievous twinkle in his eye. "The Polk was this huge theater, and it was packed to the gills for the contest, which featured many contestants, most of whom were doing similar Kingston Trio, preppy-knockoff material. Being the only Vermonter, I had other ideas and when I walked out on stage with my banjo, I hesitated, looked around at the crowd, then took a big wad of chewing gum out of my mouth and stuck it on the shiny chrome microphone stand. That rather rebellious move seemed to separate me from the other contestants and got me a huge round of applause."

Rick performed three of his amusing, slightly off-color folk songs, and the audience went nuts. It seemed to him that they'd never seen anyone quite like him before. At the end of the night, he not only took home the coveted first place prize, but also a growing sense of excitement in his ability to interact with an audience and make people laugh.

After winning the *Hootenanny Contest*, Rick was excited to be asked to play for several community events and civic clubs around the Lakeland area. By midway through the fall semester, however, he was getting a little homesick, so he decided to bring a couple of his musician friends, Bud Boydston and

Tom Azarian, down from Vermont to perform with him. In the past they had occasionally played together as a group called The New Walden Folk Singers. Not having enough money of his own to sponsor their trip, Rick convinced the freshman class to book the Vermont singers to play a concert on the campus of Florida Southern. He was able to get the school to front him $400 for the show, which covered the cost of his friends' plane tickets to Florida. In addition to the campus concert, Rick hustled up a number of other paying gigs for the group, including one at Cypress Gardens, a very popular Florida tourist attraction.

That mini-tour was the first of many times Rick created opportunities for other musicians to play and widen their experience and exposure. Though he knew he would always keep close ties with home, he also knew he wanted to learn as much about the music business as possible from professionals outside of Vermont. At age 18, barely two years after he learned how to play the guitar in Harold Patch's kitchen, Rick's career as a performer and as a music promoter had begun.

Though Rick's career was blossoming and he liked the warm Florida weather, by the time Christmas vacation arrived, he had become terribly homesick. "After growing up in the hills of Vermont, it was strange being in a landscape as flat as Florida, where the only place I could find running water was coming out of a faucet. The truth was I missed the mountains and the bright fall foliage and, most of all, the folks in Hardwick, especially Mr. Patch."

Rick took a leave from Florida Southern College after that first semester and returned to East Hardwick. "Initially, I was just glad to be home and see everyone, but then winter quickly settled in, the temperature fell well below zero, and I was in shock." Before he left school, the college chaplain had been impressed enough with Rick's musical talents that he had recommended Rick as an entertainer to his friend, Reverend Lawrence LeCour, of the Methodist Church National Board of Evangelism in Nashville, Tennessee. Rick had been in touch with Reverend LeCour, who said he would contact Rick if they were in need of a folk singer. To Rick's relief, shortly after arriving in East Hardwick, he was offered a week of work performing for the Methodist Church at a religious event at West Virginia Wesleyan College. Though it was a long haul from Vermont and Rick was far from an evangelical, he needed the money and the winter weather was getting worse.

Needing some wheels to get him to West Virginia, Rick procured the first of what he called his "farm field fleet of trucks." His friend, Bud Boydston, gave him a retired 1934 GMC flatbed farm truck that he and Rick were able to haul out of Bud's back pasture. It had no side windows or starter and the paint was mostly worn off, but they were happy to find that the stem-wind crank still worked. Rick felt it was road worthy as he couldn't see any spots where the frame was rusted all the way through. After installing a new battery, they dripped fresh gas and a little ether down into the carburetor bowl and, with some serious coaxing, were able to fire it up.

The old girl hadn't been inspected for years and wasn't close to meeting over-the-road regulations, so Rick tied a milk can on the back, mounted an agricultural plate on the grill, and took it over to Hay's Service Station, where he thought he could talk his cousin into inspecting it for him. His cousin frowned when he saw the condition of the GMC, but reluctantly agreed to put a sticker on it when Rick promised he and the dilapidated truck would be on their way to West Virginia and out of Vermont in a matter of hours.

According to a 1964 Harold Patch article in the *Hardwick Gazette*, Rick prepared to leave on his trip on the second of February, just before a snow storm was about to blow into town. Rick dressed in many layers of clothing, covered a hole in the truck's floorboard with cardboard and put a bearskin rug and a pillow over the springs protruding through the seat. He climbed in and bundled up in a blanket as best he could to shield himself from cold air blowing in through the open side windows. With his guitar and banjo in the cab with him and about ten dollars in his pocket, Rick headed out of Hardwick at two-thirty in the morning, his dim yellow headlamps illuminating the snowy road as he made his way down Route 100 through Stowe.

It was 15 below zero when he reached Burlington about five that morning. With no heater in the truck and frigid air coming in the windows, he was about frozen by the time he stopped at a filling station to gas up. For several miles the truck had been making a strange noise under the hood and when he got out to look, he saw the radiator had come loose from its mounting. He realized that it had slid down far enough that he would no longer be able to slide the crank in to restart the truck. It was so cold his body ached, but Rick knew he had to somehow fix the radiator and keep going. He got a cup of hot coffee at a nearby all-night truck stop which warmed his hands enough he was able to use them.

It was a struggle working on the radiator alone in the dark, but Rick was able to hold it up where it belonged with his shoulder so he could bolt it back onto its supports. He was finally able to slip the crank in, turn the engine over enough to start it, and head south again.

Rick only got as far as Charlotte, Vermont, before the transmission started acting up. The truck kept popping out of fourth gear and the only way he could keep going was to drive with one hand holding the stick down and the other on the wheel. He recalled, "I stopped at every gas station I came to for help, and if there was anyone inside, they all just shook their heads, swore the transmission was gone and said they couldn't help."

Not ready to give up on Bud Boydston's old GMC, Rick "crawled over the Champlain Bridge into New York at about seven miles per hour and kept hoping that at the next town there would be someone to help me out."

Crossing the bridge, the icy wind coming off Lake Champlain was nearly paralyzing, but Rick hunkered behind the windshield and slowly made his way to Ticonderoga on the New York side. There he found an empathic mechanic who figured out the transmission had come loose from the clutch and – like most everything else on the truck – was leaking oil. The man tightened the bolts and refilled the transmission oil, and Rick was off again.

Many tiring hours later, Rick arrived in Syracuse, where the truck conked out at a stop light during the evening rush hour. With a cop and an unfriendly line of vehicles behind him, Rick climbed out and crank-started the GMC again. This time, he made it a short distance out of Syracuse before the truck's engine died again. Rick pulled on another coat, got out, pushed the truck to the side of the road, and walked to a nearby service station. There he found another friendly mechanic, who installed two feet of new copper wire to replace a badly corroded piece that had shorted out the engine. He paid the man $4.50, which was about half the money he had left, picked up a college student who was hitchhiking, and headed for the Pennsylvania line.

Before long it started snowing hard, the roadway became very slick, and with just one small, vacuum-assisted windshield wiper, it was hard for Rick to see. Strong winds buffeted the truck, rattling the rusted fenders, but it held together through the storm. They made it to Binghamton, New York, about three in the morning. After 24 hours of very stressful driving, Rick was exhausted and needed some rest before traveling on.

He found a Laundromat that was open and he and his hitchhiker decided to try and get some sleep inside out of the storm and out of the frozen truck. "I pulled my bearskin rug off the seat of the truck as well as the pillow I used to sit on, and spread them out on the Laundromat floor. I immediately fell asleep and a couple of hours later woke up and realized that for some strange reason the hitchhiker had taken off on me. I couldn't imagine why. Anyway, I got a candy bar out of an old vending machine, climbed back into the truck and headed off, hoping and praying the old rig would get me through to West Virginia."

After lubricating the leaky transmission several times while crossing a snowy Pennsylvania, by Thursday morning Rick was very happy to cross the West Virginia line. He thought it a miracle he and the '34 GMC had actually made it. Rick found the richly forested Appalachian Mountains to be a lot like Vermont except he thought the state had the worst roads he'd ever seen, and

44

that's saying something coming from the Northeast Kingdom. By mid-afternoon, he arrived at Wesleyan College with considerable fanfare as the truck had finally overheated after climbing up and down several steep mountain passes. Rick remembered with a laugh, "As I drove onto campus, steam was coming out of the radiator so fast that I had to turn on the windshield wiper in order to see anything." Regardless, he was glad to be back in a warmer clime.

During that week at Wesleyan, Rick entertained with his comedic folk songs and was so well received the college asked him to stay on as a student for the spring semester. Even though he started the semester late, he was delighted at the opportunity and thus joined the freshman class. That spring, Rick spent most of his free time playing with other student musicians. He also became friends with one particularly nice fellow, a custodian at the college who lived in a humble cabin down in a holler at the foot of the mountains. After they got to know each other, the man invited Rick to his home for dinner after which he enjoyed an evening of listening to his family play Appalachian folk music around their kitchen table.

Rick appreciated learning local folk songs which deepened his ability to write and play his own music. He realized the best folk songs came straight from people's life experiences and that he was accumulating some great material of his own. Looking back, Rick didn't remember being aware of any organized plan to become a professional musician, just that he was very much living in the moment, taking in what each new day had to offer and following his gut, which more and more, led toward music in one form or another.

At the end of the school year, Rick packed up the GMC, painted "Vermont or Bust" on the door, and headed back home. Even though the weather was much better for traveling, the GMC only made it as far as western Pennsylvania before it "calved," as Rick said. Amazingly, he was able to find a local guy who ran a junkyard and was interested in the old truck. Rick traded with the guy for what Rick called a "granny car," a smooth running, 1950 Plymouth sedan that got him back to Vermont without a single breakdown.

Seeing as Rick had a predilection for old trucks, the nice sedan turned out to be a little too fancy for him. He laughed when he recalled what he did. "I soon swapped that perfectly good, reliable sedan to a farmer in Walden for a gem of a 1933 International pick-'em-up truck. It was complete with a red kerosene railroad lantern for a tail light, a spare tire roped to the fender and a milking pail tied to the rear bumper to gather water from streams when the radiator overheated."

During the summer of 1964 Rick went back to performing at the Trapp Family Lodge and was fortunate to get enough time off to go to the famed *Newport Folk Festival* in Rhode Island. The performances were held on a simple wooden stage, and Rick was excited to see many of the great musicians of the day, including a performance by Bob Dylan and Pete Seeger.

During the festival, Rick took some of his first photographs of musicians, using a Kodak Instamatic camera. "I was just blown away by the power of Dylan's performance. Generally there was so much great playing going on, both on and off the stage, you couldn't help but learn a lot and get inspired. It really moved my music development along. Back in Vermont I only had a few people to play with but at Newport there were tons of people to learn techniques from, including workshops put on by Mississippi John Hurt, "Mother" Maybelle Carter and Pete Seeger, who, sadly, I steered clear of."

In addition to his guitar and banjo, Rick had brought a handwritten letter from his friend Bud Boydston, introducing Rick to Ramblin' Jack Elliot, a popular singer and good friend of Bud's from his hosting days at Knott's Berry Farm. Elliot was a real character, whom Bud remembered driving into Knott's in a Model A Ford, steering with his feet while playing a guitar. Rick was excited to meet Elliot as he had released several records on the Folkways label and was also a good friend of folk legend, Woody Guthrie. Rick caught up with Ramblin' Jack and presented him the introductory letter from Bud Boydston. Elliot was immediately welcoming to the young singer from Vermont, and invited Rick to join him and his father for dinner, which

Rick appreciated. They enjoyed spending time together and remained friends for many years.

That summer Rick had been hired to work for the Methodist Church, so after the *Newport Folk Festival* he headed west to Lake Webster, Indiana. A Norcross road trip wouldn't be complete, however, without a little truck trouble along the way. While driving into New York City he was forced by the aggressive traffic into the wrong lane and onto the Cross Bronx Expressway, where he was pushed to speed up to 50 miles per hour. This was more than Rick's '33 International pickup could handle, and it spun a main bearing, causing the engine to knock loudly. Rick stopped and got some 50 weight motor oil – the heaviest he could find – and for the rest of the trip to Lake Webster drove under 30 miles per hour, making frequent stops to pour more oil into the engine, which allowed it to keep running.

Early in the trip, Rick stopped briefly to see his dad in Maryland, but as usual, they didn't seem to have a lot to talk about, so Rick continued on. After finally making it to Lake Webster, he spent the summer working for the Methodist Church, passing out handbills door-to-door as well as occasionally performing.

Come September, Rick left Indiana and headed back to school at Florida Southern College. Along the way, he ran out of money and had to sell his fiddle and a few other possessions to keep food in his stomach as well as oil and gas in the truck, but he made it. Once back at FSC, Rick continued his studies in English and music. He also spent as much time as possible performing, rejoining the college concert choir, with whom he had sung the year before. The choir had often toured, traveling as far as Key West in a pair of early 1950's Flxible buses. They had also performed at major civic events including memorial services for President Kennedy after he was assassinated the year before.

More and more, playing music had become the focus of Rick's life. He also developed an interest in music promotion and decided to try and find a place where he could open a coffeehouse dedicated to giving folk singers a regular place to perform. There were very few such venues in Florida but he was sure there was sufficient interest if he could find the right place for it.

Rick had become friends with the owners of Casswin's Music Store, which was located next to the FSC campus in a three-storefront building that also housed a popular eatery called, Fat Jack's Delicatessen. Rick thought the empty storefront would be a great location for a small music venue. True to form, he was able to talk the owners into letting him open a music club in the vacant space. The plan called for Casswin's to supply the music equipment and Fat Jack's to supply the food for the club's limited menu. Rick's friends helped decorate the place, hanging posters and paintings on the walls and suspending old fishnets from the ceiling. They scavenged up 15 tables and chairs and placed candles on the tables, which provided much of the small club's illumination. With a hand made sign on the front window and great enthusiasm and high hopes inside, Rick opened The Other Room Coffee House in October of 1964.

Word of the new coffeehouse quickly spread and before long it was considered the place to perform. The Other Room had an "open stage" policy, combined with several regular performers including Rick, Kayle Payne, and Sammy Schneider. There was no cover charge at the club but the singers did divide the "kitty on the wall" pot of donations at the end of each night.

Rick was also able to host visiting musicians, including Florida folk singers, Will McLean and Dash Moore. 'Waco' Jack Estes dropped in to play one night, as did Gram Parsons, who lived in nearby Winter Haven. Rick had met Parsons hanging out talking about music in Casswin's store where Rick gave guitar lessons and at one point taught Parsons how to play a Pete Seeger song on his banjo. Then, when Rick opened The Other Room, Parsons brought his folk group, The Shilohs, to Lakeland to perform. Gram Parsons went on to play with the International Submarine Band, then took the Byrds into the country-rock arena with their ground-breaking *Sweetheart of the Rodeo* album. A true musical legend known as the "Father of Country Rock," tragically, Parsons later descended into alcohol and drug addiction and died less than ten years after he performed at The Other Room.

One of Rick's favorite memories of The Other Room was the night Florida folksingers Will McLean and Dash Moore arrived in their "tour bus," a classic 1938 Lasalle hearse. Seeing the beautiful hearse parked in front of the coffeehouse was so cool Rick decided he had to have one for himself. He asked around and discovered that in Jacksonville, Florida, there was a hearse "graveyard" run by the Miller-Meteor funeral car company. Rick learned that for $150 he could go onto a lot with several hundred hearses lined up, pick out any one you wanted and drive it home. He had a blast looking over the rows and rows of retired, perfectly good hearses. He picked out a beautiful, 1955 white Cadillac, its heavy chrome, double-bullet bumpers and grill gleaming in the Florida sunshine. Feeling satisfied, Rick proudly drove back to Lakeland in the Caddy and perhaps for the first time had an inkling he was on his way to fame and fortune — of some sort, at least.

One of the great things about the coffeehouse was that people from many different walks of life came together there. One young fellow, Frank Ross, frequented The Other Room during his senior year in high school before being drafted and sent to Viet Nam. Frank looked back at those days, "What Rick did in starting that coffeehouse was huge. You have to picture back to the Sixties and for sleepy Lakeland, having a scene as cool as The Other Room, just like they had in Greenwich Village in New York, was pretty heady stuff."

Frank recognized Rick's special mix of talents, which, beyond being a fine performer, included a warm, engaging personality. He had a sense that this hick from Vermont would go far. "Rick is one of those people that always had a smile on his face and bent over backwards to help someone who needed it; a man of vision with the panache, promotional sense and chutzpah to convince important people that an idea will work. Looking back, these traits have served him well over a long and distinguished musical career, both as a performer and as a promoter." Rick and Frank later became good friends and their paths

49

would continue to cross many times over the years as they shared their mutual love of music, and eventually, photography.

Rick kept the coffeehouse going through the spring of 1965. By then he was 20 years old and constantly looking for new opportunities to perform. Over Easter week, the Methodist Church invited him to become part of the *All American All-Star Caravan* at Daytona Beach, which was overrun each April by tens of thousands of college students on vacation. The *Caravan* was a multi-faceted entertainment event put on jointly by the City of Daytona and the Methodist Church to entertain, contain, and perhaps convert some of the throngs of celebratory college students. The focus of entertainment on the beach was a flatbed truck with a palm leaf-covered stage upon which different groups of entertainers would perform. After an hour show, the truck would drive up the beach a hundred yards or so and perform essentially the same show as before for a different crowd of students.

Rick was one of the pure musical acts that entertained in between religious proselytizers, and he remembered the annual event as a beachfront carnival that somehow came off quite smoothly. One of the acts involved football player, Fran Tarkington and his evangelical "Jocks for Christ." There was also Paul Anderson, the "World's Strongest Man," who performed his amazing feat of standing in the sand and lifting a large table loaded with 20 or more students high into the air. Anderson was a world champion heavyweight lifter who won the gold medal in the 1956 Olympics for doing an astonishing and record-breaking back lift of 6,270 pounds!

One of the great musicians performing in Daytona, and the fellow who had invited Rick to play there, was a jazz pianist and accordion player named Knocky Parker, whom *Downbeat Magazine*, the bible of the jazz scene, had called the "King of the Ragtime Pianists." Parker was an early member of the Light Crust Doughboys, one of the original Texas swing bands founded in 1931 in Fort Worth, Texas by the Burrus Mills Company to promote their Light Crust Flour. Knocky, along with Smokey Montgomery, joined the Doughboys after founding member Bob Wills left the band in 1935.

The Doughboys became hugely popular particularly in the Southwest and at one time broadcast their shows on 170 different radio stations throughout the southern United States. The Doughboys also appeared in two movies including the 1936 Gene Autry film, *Oh, Susanna!* The band traveled in their own plane and custom bus, which had a stage complete with loudspeakers built into the back from which they performed their shows. The band pioneered western swing music, which had an upbeat, danceable sound which later influenced the hugely successful band, Asleep at the Wheel, and eventually, Northern New England's premier western swing band, Rick and the All Star Ramblers. Parker was also a professor of English at the University of South Florida in Tampa, which later proved fortunate for Rick.

During his sophomore year at Florida Southern College, Rick dated a girl named Virginia, daughter of the owner of several major bus lines. They had a good time together and she enjoyed listening to music at The Other Room where a lot of the *cool crowd* hung out. While he was quite enthusiastic about her, it appeared that Virginia's parents weren't quite as excited about their daughter dating a rather wild, provincial musician from the hills of Vermont. Rick said this became abundantly clear when the spring semester ended in May of 1965 and he offered to give Virginia a ride home to Charlottesville, VA, in his beautiful Cadillac hearse. When she approached her parents with the idea, they simply forbid it. As a bit of a consolation prize, however, Virginia gave Rick a few of her many possessions from college and he was allowed to drop them off at her house on his way north.

Not one to waste a road trip, Rick decided he would stop and visit some famous people he admired on his way through North Carolina. As he was studying English in college, he thought it would be fun to meet the great poet, historian, folk singer, and activist, Carl Sandburg, winner of three Pulitzer Prizes. He drove to Sandburg's hometown of Flat Rock, North Carolina, asked around, and was told where Sandburg lived. Rick headed out of town and was soon driving down the long driveway to *Connemara*, Sandburg's large estate. He got out, knocked on the front door and shortly the door swung open and a rather unwelcoming woman scowled at him from behind the screen. Rick recalled that moment, "I introduced myself as an admiring college student and a folk singer to boot, and told her I'd like to meet Mr. Sandburg. Not looking impressed, the woman sternly allowed as Mr. Sandburg was at home but would not be having any uninvited intrusions from a scraggly-haired, wannabee-poet. She pushed the screen door open right in my face, and told me to 'get out of here and go back to your own kind!' She then slammed the door and disappeared back inside."

Rick surmised the Sandburgs had seen a few too many college student wannabees, so fearing her hospitality might soon be accentuated by a load of buckshot, he jumped back into the hearse, rolled the window up and tore down the driveway.

Not wanting to give up on the idea of rubbing elbows with those who inspired him, Rick next headed to Deep Gap, North Carolina, home of the highly respected flat-picking guitarist, Doc Watson. Again, Rick asked around town for directions to Doc's house and people were happy to tell him how to get there. He soon approached the Watson's small, white-washed house that sat under a large dogwood tree. He knocked on the door and was greeted by a woman who introduced herself as Rosa Lee, Doc's wife. Seemingly at ease with Rick's somewhat scruffy appearance and the dusty white hearse in the driveway, she asked him if he'd like to come in for a cup of coffee. Delighted with her kindly reception, Rick entered her tiny kitchen, sat in a well-worn wooden chair, and they proceeded to have a wonderful conversation that lasted a couple of hours.

Rick remembered his visit with Mrs. Watson with fondness. "She told me she was home alone as Doc was off performing and their son, Merle, was on his way to a high school dance. She was the sweetest, most welcoming woman, interested in all kinds of things from music, to where I came from and what Vermont was like. She wanted to know what I was studying, what authors I was reading and what I was doing to develop my music career. She just couldn't have been nicer and was very sympathetic towards a young musician trying to make it. I think this was in part because it was just a few years before that that Doc was discovered to be a world class guitarist who came from a tiny Appalachian town."

His spirits soaring, Rick said goodbye to Mrs. Watson and headed north to say hello to Virginia and leave off her belongings. When he arrived in his muddy hearse at her opulent home in Charlottesville, he was not terribly well received. He unloaded her things and, because he was obviously exhausted, her parents let him sleep on a couch in the basement for the night. Early the next morning he was shown the door and her father made it clear – in no uncertain terms – that Rick was *never* to see his daughter again. In fact, soon after meeting Rick, he took his daughter out of Florida Southern College and sent her to school in California.

Much happier and life-changing times were waiting for the talented 20-year-old Norcross, but they would take place far from Florida and Vermont, or as he said, "across the big pond."

Chapter Five

BRITAIN BOUND

Since his high school days, Rick had enjoyed *Sing Out Magazine,* a popular folk music journal. One article interested him in particular, in which Pete Seeger wrote about performing in the vibrant folk scene in England. He talked about how warmly the Brits welcomed American musicians and recounted what a good time he had playing with fellow American, Arlo Guthrie at the Troubadour Club in London. Seeger and other major artists played mostly large concert halls in the cities, but there was also an extensive network of small folk clubs all over England in what local pubs called their *community rooms.* Most professional folk musicians lived in London and traveled by train to play these clubs, where they were received by the locals with great enthusiasm. Rick was attracted to the English folk scene, as playing intimate clubs was what he enjoyed most.

On his ride up from North Carolina, Rick decided a trip to England would benefit his singing and songwriting career more than staying in the U.S. After he arrived home in East Hardwick in late May of 1965, he parked the white Caddy in his Grandmother Delilah's yard and told her of his plans to set sail for England. She and some of her friends thought Rick was crazy for wanting to go across the Atlantic Ocean just to sing, but as the time for him to leave neared, they began to share his excitement. Mr. Patch, for one, thought it would be a great adventure.

Rick asked his grandmother if he could leave the hearse parked in her yard, and she reluctantly agreed. He then scraped enough money together to buy a $237 ticket for a voyage from Montreal to Liverpool, England, aboard the ocean liner, *The Empress of England*. The ship was the largest he'd ever seen, holding about a thousand passengers, most of whom were young women college students heading for guided tours of England and Europe for the summer. Rick recalled having a great time until, halfway across the Atlantic, he was informed the only way he would be allowed to get off the ship and set foot on British soil was if he: a) held a round trip ticket (which he did not), or b) had at least $200 on his person (he had barely $35). One of the tour guides on the ship told him that otherwise the authorities would not let him disembark and they would return him to Canada on the next ship sailing west.

Crestfallen, but ever-resourceful, Rick was determined to make it to the London folk scene. He asked one of the tour's chaperones for help and was told they were about to hold a talent show aboard the ship, so Rick signed up and played several songs. The other students found him to be an amusing and talented entertainer, and decided to help him get through customs.

When they arrived at the port of Liverpool, the leader of the tour told Rick to walk right along with all of the other students as they went through the group processing queue, which assumed they all had their round trip tickets in order. Knowing full well his friends were helping him break international immigration law, Rick was a tad nervous as they prepared to disembark in front of British officials. Rick played the part beautifully and no one questioned him as he walked off the ship in the middle of the group of students and proceeded past a cadre of stern-faced immigration officers. Soon he was boarding the train that would take him from Liverpool to London, a prized six-month tourist visa held tightly in his hand.

Rick arrived in London the same weekend as the *Wimbledon Tennis Tournament* and the world convention of the Salvation Army. Anxious to try and connect with the folk scene he had been reading about, he headed in the direction of the famed Troubadour Club, located on Old Brompton Road in the Earls Court section of southwest London. A small club framed with leaded glass windows filled with shelves of colorful vintage coffee pots, the Troubadour had continuously hosted music since its founding in 1954. Since then its stage has been graced by great musical legends including Richard Harris, Charlie Watts, Bob Dylan, Paul Simon, Jimmy Page, Robert Plant, and Jimi Hendrix.

Rick took a good look at the Troubadour then walked down to Brompton Road, where he spent his first night in a clean, but quite Spartan German Youth Hostel. The next day, with very little money left in his pocket, Rick kept exploring, and found a "wicked cheap room in a cold water walkup." He recalled that the place was in a pretty seedy section of the city, but it was the best he could afford. Fortunately, he had a couple of hundred US pennies with him that he had tossed into his banjo case over the years. He quickly figured out that they were the same size as the British six pence coin. "Those copper pennies were a godsend as they fit in the Tube turnstiles, the pay telephones, and most importantly, in the Cadbury Fruit and Nut Bar and orange juice vending machines. Alone in a foreign land, those old pennies literally saved my life." He later learned British officials forbid American servicemen stationed in England from possessing US pennies for obvious reasons. It was a good thing he hadn't worn his Shelburne Junior Marine Corp uniform over there or they might have caught him.

Knowing he had to make some quick money to survive, Rick found a copy of London's music newspaper, *The Melody Maker,* and checked out the local folk listings. He figured he might as well give it a shot at the best folk club around, so that evening he went back to the Troubadour and met manager, Redd Sullivan. Rick gave him the skinny on who he was and the kind of music he played, which at that point was mostly his original songs as well as comedic folk parodies. Redd had had good experiences with American folk singers and was kind and receptive to Rick. In fact, Rick was delighted and relieved when Redd gave him a "floor singer spot," which meant Rick went on before the main act and did a couple of songs. The first night his performance was so well received Redd asked him to start performing at the club on a regular basis.

In the audience at the Troubadour there were often people from outside London who owned or were involved in the network of local folk clubs that dotted the English countryside. As Seeger had written, such clubs were often in the backroom of local pubs, and were extremely popular. Rick's engaging personality and his rather unique American folk style prompted many invitations to travel by train to perform in small towns all over England. He soon realized he needed a booking agent to handle his expanding performance schedule and was referred to Graham Wood at the London City Agency. Rick was pleased as Wood was also the agent for another young American folk singer from New York, Paul Simon. With Wood's help, Rick became a popular headliner, and the more he played the more work he got.

At that time folk performances were acoustic without any sound systems, and the audiences were attentive and receptive. Rick remembered those early days in England, "I couldn't believe how easy it was to work in the clubs over there. With floor singers doing part of the show and clubs required to close by 10:30 pm, the headliners only did a couple of 30 minute slots, allowing me to do only my best material, which really went over well with the audiences. This was so much better for a performer than in the US where we did three or four grueling, hour-long sets of music, which was just brutal. It was so cool back then with the closeness of the musicians with the audience and with each other. We were all hanging out enjoying music together like normal people; nothing like it is now with huge separations between big celebrity performers and the audience.

"In fact, I remember in November of 1965, I played a folk club in Bedford and that evening Doc Watson was headlining and I was the opener. Between his sets, I sat and talked with Doc and relayed the story of stopping by his house in Deep Gap the spring before and my wonderful visit with his wife, Rosa Lee. Like his wife, he was so gracious to me, sharing his own experiences and showing sincere interest in what I was doing. That was the sort of thing that happened naturally back then. As time went on, performers have had to deal with big sound systems, light shows, huge stages and artists' reps to get through and connect with the audience. I think that simpler time in the Sixties was so great for me as my original folk and comedic material best lends itself to being performed in those small club and house concert type situations. Not that it wasn't a blast to play in front of 40,000 people, which I did many years later at Tampa Stadium at a United States Football League event."

One of Rick's favorite parts of the English folk scene was that many of the musicians lived in London and returned to the city by train late at night after going out to their gigs in the small towns. On Saturday nights there was one all-night folk club, Les Cousins on Greek Street in the SOHO District, which hosted a midnight-to-dawn show. One of the musicians that performed there regularly was a fellow named, Diz Disley, a very accomplished jazz musician who, when the popularity of jazz waned, had started doing his own folk act. Rick and Diz met at a show during the fall of 1965, and both being comedic performers, enjoyed each other's acts and started hanging out together.

"Diz was outrageously funny on stage: eccentric, hilarious and usually drunk, to the point where he would often show up to gigs late or not at all. And sometimes he'd forget to bring his guitar with him. But audiences loved him and the time I spent with him back then was great. He was a well known jazz player and I met many of his jazz musician friends in England, even though by then he was doing a lot of his comedic shows. Diz was a huge influence on me."

William Charles "Diz" Disley was born in Manitoba, Canada where his Welch-born father had moved his family so he could work there as a laborer. Soon after Diz was born, however, the family moved back to Wales and later to Yorkshire, England, where Diz eventually attended Leeds College of Art, becoming a reputed cartoonist and illustrator. While studying at Leeds he was befriended by a musician named Norry Greenwood, who turned Diz onto the music of gypsy musician, Django Reinhardt. Diz wrote that it was "the genius of this great man" that brought him to music. Revering the work of Reinhardt, Diz became an extremely accomplished guitar and banjo player and performed in jazz bands for many years until he transitioned into the British folk scene in the mid Sixties, which was when he met Rick. At that time Rick was trying to find a better place to live than the cold water walk-up he'd been renting, so Diz introduced him to Hylda Simms, the woman who owned the boarding house where he lived in West Dulwich. Simms rented a spare room to Rick, and he and Diz became good friends.

Disley was not only a very popular performer, he was quite a character as well. Rick recalled one day Diz picked Rick up in his 1928 Red Label Rolls Royce and they drove to the headquarters of the BBC, where Diz was going to pick up a royalty check for some work he had done. "Diz parks his Rolls right in front of the building and with some fanfare, we walked up to the main door and at that moment two guys in full monk's habits are walking out. They had big hoods, floor length velvet robes, the whole nine yards. When they looked up and recognized Diz, they got all excited and started yelling, 'Halloooo – Disley!' They grabbed him and started pumping his hand in a rather wild greeting, all of which seemed to delight Diz and garnered the attention of a number of people passing by. When their hoods came off, I realized the monks were actually the great British comedians Peter Cook and Dudley Moore. Diz introduced me, we had a quick visit, and then we all continued on like nothing had happened. That was pretty typical of a day hanging out with Diz."

Rick remembered that Diz often came up with bizarre get-rich-quick schemes. One memorable idea involved jam-packing a vintage Rolls Royce with hundreds of Elizabethan chamber pots and shipping them to New York City where he was sure he could make a killing selling them to antique shops. Diz said the plan couldn't fail as he could buy piles of the old pots for pennies apiece in England and he was sure that collectors in the U.S. would love them. Rick thought the idea was a little crazy and never found out if Diz pulled that one off, but he doubted it.

One of the larger English music clubs was the Surbiton and Kingston Folk Club, which held its concerts in a large function hall complex called The Assembly Rooms. One evening at a concert, Diz introduced Rick to a friend and fellow musician who ran the club named, Derek Sarjeant. Sarjeant was a major force in the English folk scene, and Rick was delighted to be invited to perform a couple of songs as a floor singer in between the main, scheduled acts.

Sarjeant recalled that evening vividly, "This young Rick Norcross fellow was very self-assured and witty on stage, and the audience took to him so well he received thunderous applause. Because of his reception, Rick ended up singing several of his self-penned songs, including, "The Universal Pacifist," a parody of Buffy St. Marie's song, "The Universal Soldier." I finally got him off the stage only by giving a public promise to book him at an early date as a featured guest artist, which I did several times during 1965 and 1966 to great receptions. During that time Rick had really made an impact on the mushrooming British folk club scene and was in great demand. In fact, Rick was so popular that I later helped arrange another solo tour for him in clubs in England and Wales when he performed with instrumentalist Pete Yorkunas. He again was very warmly received."

Playing the popular Assembly Rooms was great exposure for Rick as Derek's club headlined some of the biggest international names in folk music, including Tom Paxton, Donovan, Doc Watson, and Long John Baldry. One night in particular Rick and Diz were asked to do some opening songs for a touring American singer, Carolyn Hester, who, along with Joan Baez and Judy Collins, were the *big three* female folk artists of the mid-Sixties. Carolyn and Rick hit it off personally and loved each other's songs. Their meeting that night began a remarkable friendship, and when they later returned to the States, Carolyn urged Rick to keep in touch, becoming a mentor for him as he tried to work his way into the big time music business.

Derek also became a good friend and supporter and played a part in helping Rick become an internationally known folk singer. Derek continued to feature Rick in his clubs when he returned to England in 1968 and 1974. Rick eventually brought Diz to the States to play in one of his Florida coffeehouses. But in the end, Rick told me that Diz turned on him in a way that could have ended Rick's British music career.

By the summer of 1965, at age 21, Rick had become popular enough that his agent got him a booking at the prestigious Stevenage Folk Festival. By then, Rick had built a reputation as a refreshing, new type of folk performer, admittedly much wilder than the traditional English artist. He would do hysterical parodies of classic songs, tell outrageous stories and loved to get the audience involved in the show. Often his final number involved leading different sections of the audience in singing three different songs all at the same time such as, "When the Saints Go Marching In," "The Crawdad Song," and "This Train." According to Derek, Rick's performances were so funny he usually left the audience begging for more. They simply had never before seen a performer like him. Following another of Rick's performances in Cambridge, Mike Seeger, a member of the New Lost City Ramblers and Pete Seeger's half-brother, told Rick that his "was the best parody of a group sing-along he had ever seen."

Unbeknownst to Rick, in the audience that day at Stevenage, was a fellow named Hugh Aldous, organizer of one of the largest folk clubs in England. Hugh and his wife, Nancy, were musicians and founders of the "Bedford Clangers," a successful club that had over 1200 members and up until that point had featured only traditional folk artists. By that summer, however, they felt the need to broaden the scope of their club's performances if they were to maintain their premier national status. Hugh decided to attend the Stevenage Festival to see what new artists might be available for hire. He never guessed who he was about to discover.

Hugh fondly recalled that day. "I attended this concert at Stevenage and was, along with the rest of the audience, absolutely amazed at a performance given by one of the relatively unknown support artists named Rick Norcross. He was a long-haired, bearded, very personable American who absolutely stole the show with his comedic performance. He was so funny and engaging he brought the house down and the audience simply refused to let him leave until after they'd made him do several encores. I cannot even remember who the main artist was; such was the effect Rick had on all of us that were there." (The main act was Bill Clifton, *the* most famous bluegrass player in England.)

Hugh, like Derek Sarjeant, knew a great entertainer when he saw one, so he approached Rick after the show and booked him into one of his concerts which was to take place a few weeks later. "When we showcased Rick in our club, he simply stole the show and again the audience would not let him leave the stage, much to the annoyance of the other performers. My wife and I became very fond of Rick and let him live and work out of our house for several months, which was a delightful experience."

As Hugh was the booking secretary for his club as well as five others, he regularly transported Rick and other musicians back and forth to the shows, often letting them stay at his home. Spending so much time with his new American friend was one of Hugh's favorite experiences during those club years. "Everywhere Rick performed he was like a breath of fresh American air in what had become a rather dull, traditional folk scene. We feel he was partly responsible for the expansion of the popular contemporary folk scene from America that flourished after his arrival on British shores."

Looking back, Rick remembered feeling really comfortable on stage at Stevenage and that he put on "a hellova show." It felt even better when he was approached after the concert by John Bailey, a luthier from London who was a highly respected guitar builder. Bailey was so impressed with Rick's imaginative performance he told Rick he thought he was going to be a big star and offered to make him a custom guitar for free if Rick simply promised to play it on stage in public performances. Rick was surprised and honored at Bailey's offer, which he gratefully accepted.

Always wanting to do something a little different than the mainstream, Rick then had the wild idea he would like to have the world's first 18-string guitar, so he asked Bailey if he could build such an instrument. Bailey had never heard of a guitar with that many strings but said he would figure out how to do it. Before long, Rick was presented with what may still be the only 18-string guitar in the world. It became his signature and he enjoyed performing with it for many years until it final wore out and became too brittle to be played.

During that busy summer of 1965, Rick also signed his first recording deal with Look Records based in Wales. Though Rick worked hard on recordings for an album, when the sessions were finished and the record mastered, it wasn't felt to be of high enough quality and thus was never released.

As his music career gained steam, Rick became very comfortable with himself, though sometimes his growing ego got in his way. At the Stevenage festival Rick's on-stage behavior actually got him in some trouble. Bill Leader, owner of Transatlantic Records had set up recording equipment at the front of the stage that day but had not asked Rick's permission to record his performance. In light of his recent successes, Rick was feeling his oats and, being a fiercely independent Vermonter, wouldn't allow his performance to be recorded.

"When I came on stage, I walked right down around in front of all his mikes and stood at the very edge of the stage, as close to the audience as I could get. That guy couldn't record a word of my show and the audience loved my defiance – like when I stuck the wad of chewing gum on the mike stand in Florida. But it pissed Leader off so badly he barely ever spoke to me again after that incident. I later regretted my behavior as things fell through with Look Records and I might have had a chance with Transatlantic if I hadn't done that. Back then I'd developed this independent persona and didn't care what people in authority thought, particularly if I felt someone was trying to take advantage of me. I'd had enough of that BS growing up. I think that's when I first started feeling like, *I'm from Vermont and I do what I want!* And 50 years later, I still have those words printed on my band's T-shirts."

By November, Rick technically should have left England as he had been granted only a six month visitor's visa. However, he had two problems with leaving. First, he was having an absolute blast as a popular member of the British folk scene. And second, making around ten pounds Sterling a night performing (about $18 US), he hadn't been able to eat, pay rent *and* save up enough money to buy a ticket home. Thus Rick enlisted his agent's assistance to find a way he could legally stay longer, and the agent was able to book Rick into a couple of week-long singing engagements in Ireland and Holland. When Rick returned to England he was able to procure a new, six-month visitor's visa, which lasted until he finally went home the following March.

Some of the most memorable experiences for Rick during his first visit to England were the times he spent with Paul Simon, who the year before, had released his first album with Art Garfunkel entitled, *Wednesday Morning, 3 AM.* The album was only available in the States and had not done particularly well, receiving little in the way of enthusiastic reviews or airplay. Simon, like Rick, had gone to England to be part of what seemed to be the world's most vibrant folk scene. Rick remembered that time well. "Paul was certainly one of the favorites around the London scene with his excellent original songs and his polished New York delivery. Because Paul and I worked out of the same agency I had the opportunity to see him quite often. Sometimes we would go out to a gig on the train together and I'd play a few opening songs before him and we'd get to talk about song writing and guitar techniques, those sorts of things. Paul used his own two-finger picking method which I'd never seen before and he thought because of that unusual style his record producers back in the States would not be able to fit drums behind his songs; something he, as a folk purist, was against. Paul was kind of a prickly guy — very precise, not warm and fuzzy — but I had great respect for him and appreciated what I learned hanging out together. And of course he was mistaken about his music not fitting drum tracks."

Ironically and unbeknownst to Simon, that fall his producer at Columbia records took his folk song, "Sounds of Silence," and overdubbed his original acoustic track with drums and electric guitars and released it as a single. The new release caught on and quickly rose up the charts, becoming Simon and Garfunkel's first number one record. Rick remembered Paul being very upset at what they had done to his quiet, reflective song without his permission. "Soon Columbia was pressuring Paul to return to New York to promote his hit record in the States, but he was not happy and held out until February 1966 when he finally decided he had to go home.

"Paul was very popular in London and when word got out that he was leaving for the States, people were happy for him but disappointed to see him go. It turned out that his final appearance in England was during one of the all-night music sessions at Les Cousins Club in London and that particular Saturday night I was booked as the host for the event. The place was completely packed with even more musicians than usual, and it was exciting and quite an honor to host Paul's going away show. I respected him for not only playing some of his great songs that night, but for also speaking honestly to the audience about his feelings of resentment around his record company messing with his folk songs." Though Rick followed Paul's career with interest, that farewell night in London was the last time Rick saw or talked with him.

While in England, not only did Rick's music career take a major leap forward, the whole experience enriched other aspects of his life. He developed a self confidence that, the majority of the time, served him well as a performer. He also learned the value of being not just a singer, but an all round *entertainer*, part of which was creating a uniquely recognizable look for when he was on stage. To accomplish this, one Saturday Rick walked to the Portobello Road flea market in London and found a sharp-looking, British military band uniform jacket, which he was able to purchase for five pounds. He wore that jacket every time he performed until late 1967, when the Beatles released their *Sgt. Peppers Lonely Hearts Club Band* album. Because the Beatles were dressed in the same kind of military band jackets, Rick decided to stop wearing his to avoid being perceived as a copycat, even though he started wearing his first.

Being in England also deepened Rick's love of history, inspired by growing up at the Shelburne Museum and nurtured by spending time with Harold Patch and his contemporaries in East Hardwick. During his time in the English countryside, Rick performed at many far-flung bookings which included lodging at the organizers' homes. They often directed Rick toward nearby castles and other historic places he enjoyed visiting. He found English history fascinating and was always looking for another site to visit.

During his later 1974 English tour, Rick and his cohort, Pete Yorkunas, stopped and visited the venerable Stonehenge on their way back to London from gigs in Cornwell and Devon. "I'll never forget that early Monday morning when we pulled up to those huge gray monoliths. There was nobody there but us, standing in the mist with that spooky wind that blows over the Salisbury Plain. And back then there were no fences so we were able to walk right in among those massive, imposing stones with their very strong, ancient presence. It's a very strange place."

Probably the only real drag during Rick's year in England was the persistence of his nasty dermatitis. As in his early days in Shelburne, at times the incessant itching and scratching got so bad he had to be admitted to the U. S. Air Force Base Hospital at Ruislip for treatment, sometimes for two weeks at a time. He was able to get care there because he was still covered by his father's military insurance. Rick recalled, "The military doctors and nurses seemed fascinated by this long-haired, American folk singer with this wicked rash. Of course I was stubborn and wouldn't go into the hospital until I was sick enough that I couldn't stand it anymore and, thankfully, they were very kind to me.

"After having to be sedated for intensive treatments, the rash would start to subside and the first thing I wanted to do was play my guitar and sing again. They liked my off-color folk songs and must have gotten a kick out of me because they'd even bring people by my hospital room to hear me play from my bed." Grinning, Rick added, "That's how I met and dated one of the general's very good looking daughters for a while."

Rick was appreciative of the care and TLC that he received at Ruislip, as well as their enthusiasm for his music career. Sometimes, if he felt able, his doctors even let him go out on pass for the evening if a gig came up. It seems that by then Rick Norcross could charm about anybody into anything.

Despite the fun he was having, by March of 1966, Rick was again homesick for Vermont and had saved up enough money to fly back to the States. Encouraged by how enthusiastically he had been received in England, and particularly by Carolyn Hester's interest in his music, Rick returned to America ready to continue building his career. "England was *so* good to me," he said, looking back, "but it was great to be heading home."

Chapter Six

BACK IN THE USA

Rick flew from London's Heathrow Airport to Montreal in March of 1966, full of excitement from his experiences in England. Though he was nearly 21 and largely living on the opportunities of each day, the prospect of making it big in the music business was taking hold. When he arrived in East Hardwick, it was a very different world than the energetic clubs of London, but Rick sure thought it was a pretty sight to see his '55 Caddy parked in his grandmother's yard. Rick was already booked for a return engagement at the Daytona Beach *All American All Star Caravan* over Easter, so he quickly rounded up some gigs in Vermont to make some money during the few weeks in between. In the Burlington area he was hired to perform shows at The Third Thumb Club in Winooski and at a fraternity party at the University of Vermont's Acacia House.

It was at the fraternity show that Rick met a beautiful local girl named Harlaine "Holly" Dudley, who caught his eye while he was on stage singing. Many years later, Holly recalled that night, "A girlfriend and I walked into this frat party and there on stage was this bushy, red-orange haired guy playing his own songs who was just back from touring in England. He was quite a memorable sight as he was wearing a fancy, navy blue wool jacket and was a great performer despite the fact that he was sweating, itching and scratching himself while singing. I just remember him being very impressive and great with the audience. You could tell right away that he was a nice, authentic guy – a real original talent. When we met after the show, he turned out to be a true gentleman, so how could you not love the guy?"

Rick and Holly sort of dated for a while that spring, during which time Rick took her home to visit his family. She distinctly remembered him picking her up at her parents' house in his white Caddy hearse and driving her along winding roads to East Hardwick for his 21st birthday party at local artist, Hazel Hall Rochester's studio. They also visited a rundown farmhouse at the end of a long dirt road in Cabot where Rick's friends, Tom and Mary Azarian, lived. Tom was one of the musician friends Rick had brought down to Florida to play as part of the New Walden Folk Singers and at that time, the wonderfully creative Mary was on her way to becoming an internationally known woodcut artist.

"I remember," Holly recalled, "when we finally got up to the farmhouse, Mary was making a steaming pot of stew on the cook stove and their baby, Ethan, was happily crawling around playing on the wood plank floor. Tom was a fine fiddler and we were psyched that he played for us before dinner. We all had a great time together then we went back to Rick's grandmother's house in East Hardwick, and I remember sleeping in her extraordinary feather bed – like nothing I'd ever been in before." She smiled. "I think Rick tried to get in with me and I kicked him out! He's always respected everything and everyone; it's just his everyday behavior."

A devotee of his music, Holly and Rick became lifelong friends. Holly and her husband, Bobby Miller, have since hired Rick and the Ramblers to play for an occasional birthday bash on the *Northern Lights*, a tour boat on Lake Champlain, plying the same waters that the great *Ticonderoga* traveled long before.

In April of 1966, before Rick left Vermont for Daytona, he spent as much time as he could with his mentor and friend, Harold Patch. He also drove to

Essex Junction to visit his beloved eighth grade teacher, Becky Blanchard, and her husband, Rene, who had been especially supportive of Rick during those difficult early days in Shelburne.

Becky recalled that visit with a smile. "Ricky had just come back from playing folk music in Europe and one day there was a big bang on the front door and this kind of wild, bearded fellow in thick granny glasses was standing there, and he was driving a white hearse. My husband was a bit alarmed and wasn't going to let the man in till he recognized that irresistible twinkle in those eyes of his. Ricky broke out in a smile, came in and gave us a big hug. We all laughed and caught up for a while then he took us out for a great ride in that huge hearse of his, which he said he needed so he could carry all his musical gear around when he played.

"It was *so* good to see him again and to know he still wanted to share his life with us. You see, part of Ricky's charm is he doesn't really realize where he's been, how far he's taken his dreams or how truly unique his life is. We've always appreciated his thoughtfulness in keeping in touch with us. It's let us old country folk be a part of his life among the famous."

As Easter week approached, Rick headed south toward Daytona for his second appearance at the *Caravan*. He was happy that his cousin Charlie had taken good care of the Caddy while he was in England *until* he was crossing over the top of the Delaware Memorial Bridge and suddenly there was a loud bang under the hood, followed by a deafening tapping noise as the engine threw a rod. Rick figured Charlie had drained the water from the radiator before the winter but had neglected to drain the block, which had frozen and cracked. The beautiful rig died coming off the bridge just before the toll booth. A highway department truck soon came up behind Rick and pushed him right up to the toll booth collector. Rick wasn't too thrilled to have to pay the toll as he technically didn't *drive* all the way over the bridge, but he paid it anyway. Then the state truck proceeded to give him another, unceremonious shove that landed the Caddy well off the side of the road.

71

Realizing it was the end of the line, Rick said good-bye to his moribund hearse then found a payphone and called his dad for help. He drove over and picked Rick up and gave him a ride to a bus stop where he caught a Greyhound bus all the way to Daytona. After playing the *Caravan* over Easter, Rick headed back north to New York City, where he had made arrangements to visit his new friend, Carolyn Hester. He was very excited as she had just returned from performing at the *Philadelphia Folk Festival* where she showcased one of Rick's songs, "Vietnam Bound," an edgy parody of Paul Simon's classic, "Homeward Bound."

Carolyn was kind enough to let Rick stay at her apartment, which was great for him because he only had about $20 left to his name. By then, Hester was one of the biggest female folk singers around, so it was a huge break for Rick when she offered to take him around to meet several of her major contacts in the recording industry, including producers John Hammond, Sr. and Milt Okun. Okun was a powerful independent record producer who had recently put together the folk trio Peter, Paul and Mary. In fact, he had offered Carolyn Hester the female position, but her own career was doing so well she elected to stay a solo act. Working as one of the most successful and influential producers of the day, Okun produced hit songs for John Denver, Placida Domingo, Harry Belafonte, the Irish Rovers and many other major artists. Over his long career he produced 75 gold and platinum records and received 16 Grammy nominations.

During a couple of meetings, Okun was impressed enough with Rick's original material, and with how well he'd been received in England, that by early May he offered Rick a preliminary record deal. They agreed that Rick would keep performing and developing his own folk material and return to meet with Okun at the end of the summer with enough songs for a full album, and then they would move forward with recording.

Despite the excitement of the looming record deal, Rick's most immediate problem was being dead broke again, so he went to work booking more gigs.

Hester was about to leave for Rhode Island, where she was hosting a song-writer's workshop at the *Newport Folk Festival*, and she invited Rick to go with her and sing his "Vietnam Bound" song as part of the workshop. Appearing with Hester at the biggest folk festival in the country was great exposure for Rick, and again, he loved being in the middle of all that creative energy. The biggest surprise, and cause for concern at the festival, was that for the first time Bob Dylan *went electric*, playing his songs on an electric guitar, which in those days was heresy in the world of folk music.

Once back in New York, Carolyn prepared to leave for a summer tour in Europe. She offered to let Rick stay in her apartment as long as he was in the city. Rick recalled, "She was unbelievably kind and welcoming to me, a true caring mentor who did everything she could to welcome me into the fold and help my career take off. I will never forget the way she treated me. But as humble as she was, I still knew I was in the presence of folk royalty. The first night I stayed in her apartment, I saw a framed hand-written scrap of paper on the wall that read: "Thanks for letting me stay overnight, Bob Dylan." It turned out Dylan had been discovered through Carolyn when she hired him as a harmonica player on her third album for Columbia in 1961. Her producer, John Hammond, Sr., was so impressed with Dylan's talents he signed him to Columbia Records. The rest, as they say, is history.

Rick and Carolyn's friendship grew and they spent a fair amount of time together that summer in New York. One experience in particular left an indelible mark on Rick. The weekend before she was to fly to Europe on tour, Carolyn received the news that her ex-husband, Richard Farina (who'd recently married Joan Baez' sister) had been killed on his motorcycle in California. Later that day, Carolyn had a strange and frightening experience riding in a cab in Manhattan. When the taxi stopped for a red light, Carolyn looked out her window and saw a black motorcycle running in the lane next to her with nobody on it. Rick recalled, "The sight of that riderless motorcycle freaked Carolyn out pretty badly. It was definitely weird."

Carolyn was booked to play the prestigious Club 47 in Harvard Square the next night. Feeling shaken by Richard's death and the sight of the black riderless motorcycle, she asked Rick to fly up to Boston and perform on the same bill with her. Club 47 was an important music venue during the Sixties folk boom and Rick felt honored to be asked to play there. On the plane they sat with Judy Collins, who was also playing in the Boston area that weekend. Later that night, after their show, Rick and Carolyn went out to dinner at the Red Fez Restaurant with Joni Mitchell, Tom Rush, and the publisher of the *Boston Phoenix* newspaper. Rush had recently recorded Mitchell's "Circle Game," which was a big success and before long she was signed by Reprise Records. Rick appreciated the opportunity to be in the company of such gifted and famous artists, all of whom were friendly and treated him with respect, encouraging him to keep working to build his own career.

After Carolyn left for Europe, Rick knew he should be working on writing new songs, but instead hit the streets looking for enough work to survive in New York. One night when he was hanging out in the West Village, he ran into his old friend, Gram Parsons, who was in town recording a record at Columbia with his group, the International Submarine Band. They went up to the Tin Angel and had a few drinks and talked about the music scene. After awhile, Gram had to take off and inadvertently left the check with Rick, who barely had enough money in his pockets to pay the bill.

Rick shook his head thinking back to those days. "That summer I was so broke I survived by literally eating everything edible in Carolyn's apartment. At one point, I actually boiled a pot of prune pits after I'd eaten the prunes so that I could drink the juice. Even the mice in the building were starving to death by the time I left. Luckily, I soon got a gig at the Gaslight Club in Manhattan opening for John Hammond, Jr. It paid five bucks a night, which was a lot more than I had in my pocket."

Rick had a funny sort of Yankee pride that, at times, undermined his ability to both survive *and* thrive, and that summer in New York was a good example.

There were opportunities in the city where musicians could play at what were called "basket houses," where musicians split the proceeds of a basket that was passed around during the night. Generally, Rick wouldn't let himself take advantage of those opportunities. "Perhaps because of my success in England, I just couldn't bring myself to play in those smoky joints, which I saw as the bottom-of-the-barrel gigs. I felt I was above it, despite the fact I was boiling prune pits and eating crumbs in Carolyn's apartment. I've never really been able to put the money thing together with the reality of my life as a musician. I've always lived on the edge financially, just barely pulling along with enough to survive, keep a decent roof over my head and be able to keep playing music. That's always been the thing — *keep the music going*." Rick added with a grin, "Now I'm 68 and no longer looking for fame and fortune. I'm just trying to find 15 minutes of fame and *solvency!*"

Despite being offered the record deal, Rick didn't exactly buckle down and start writing more songs as Okun had required to seal their upcoming record deal. "Part of the problem with my material was that much of it was really written for folk club-type performances and just didn't lend itself that well to recording. Plus, I'd only been writing for a few years and still had a lot of maturing to do as an artist. Looking back, I should have put a lot more energy into working on new songs instead of trying to get the next gig. But I was broke and was more focused on the immediate thing in front of me — like eating — rather than what I needed to do to meet the requirements of the record deal by the end of that summer."

Even though he was able to land a few gigs, Rick realized he couldn't afford to stay in New York and thus connected with a booking agent in Massachusetts named Dick Waterman, whom he had met at the *Newport Folk Festival* with Hester. Waterman represented big artists like Bonnie Raitt and Mississippi John Hurt and was able to get Rick a week-long gig at the Pesky Sarpent, a popular coffeehouse built in a converted subterranean bowling alley in Springfield, Massachusetts. Rick was psyched as the Sarpent showcased a lot of well known folk acts including Arlo Guthrie and Don McLean.

When he arrived by bus in Springfield, however, his welcome was not a warm one. Rick recalled, "Looking like a sketchy hippie, when I stepped off the bus I was immediately hassled by a couple of Springfield police officers who demanded to see my draft card, which I never carried as I was classified as a lowly *1-F*. A fellow at the American Embassy in London had previously told me that classification was so low the military would take women and children before they'd take me. I think with all the times I'd been in military hospitals for the dermatitis and the fact I was allergic to wool, the government had already spent too much on me and wanted to cut their losses."

Despite not having his draft card with him, Rick talked his way out of the situation and headed to the Sarpent, where his performances were so enthusiastically received he was given the manager's job and spent the rest of the summer working there. In addition, as much as time would allow, he drove back and forth to Vermont and New York, seeing friends, making contacts and playing as many gigs as possible.

Some nights when Rick was in New York, he'd stay on the couch of a fellow named Israel "Izzy" Young, who ran a music store called The Folk Center, located above the Waverly Theater on the Avenue of the Americas. Rick remembered Izzy with admiration, "He was a legend among folksingers of the day and his apartment was like the crossroads for musicians in New York. He let them hang out and sleep on his couch all the time for free and I remember those nights well because the couch was under a window that was right next to the bright neon, blinking marquee for the Waverly Theater downstairs. It was hard to sleep, but I was grateful to Izzy for giving so many of us a place to crash and often a bite to eat. His was a vibrant, artsy neighborhood that most of the time kept going all night. It was a very cool place to be as great musicians like Dave van Ronk lived right around the corner."

Despite his financial woes, toward the end of the summer Rick got a hankering for a new set of wheels. When he had played Daytona earlier that spring he'd met some college guys from New Hampshire who had driven down in a beautiful 1937 Packard hearse and Rick had kept in touch with them. At one point he heard that they were ready to sell the Packard and he *really* wanted to buy it, but couldn't put together the $600 they wanted for it. So he came up with a novel idea to pay for it. Carolyn had recently offered to sign Rick to her own music publishing company, Crazy Creek Music. By the time she returned from her European tour, Rick told her he was ready to sign and wondered if she might buy him the hearse as his signing payment. Hester appreciated Rick's eccentricities and got a kick out of him, so she bought him the hearse and he was soon driving around in his new '37 Packard. Rick fell in love with the jet black beauty, though it was so long it took up two parking spaces and the engine needed a major overhaul. Rick worked more gigs, and scrimped and saved every penny he could to get the engine job done before heading south to Florida in September.

By then it was time to meet with Okun again, hopefully to complete their record deal. Unfortunately, a lot had changed in the music business over that summer. In addition to Rick undermining himself by not writing enough new songs, the bottom had fallen out of the commercial folk market, largely due to Dylan's huge influence in *going electric* at Newport. In general, record companies were not signing new folk acts, and were actually abandoning projects already underway. Needless to say, Rick's deal never materialized.

By the fall of 1966, Rick headed back to school. Because of all of his musical touring and travel, he was only a sophomore, but was committed to working on his college degree. He went to pick up the repaired Packard but was $70 short on the bill, and the mechanic wasn't very happy. Rick talked him into letting him take the car anyway, promising to send the man the balance as soon as he could. Rick loaded up the hearse with his guitars and other gear and headed out. By then his eyesight was failing badly, a result of worsening cataracts that had developed from his cortisone treatment for the chronic dermatitis. At times his vision was so blurry the only way he could drive was to follow closely behind another vehicle, stopping and going in synch with their taillights. Occasionally, he missed an exit on the interstate and got lost. As he was unable to read many of the road signs, it was a very frustrating experience finding his way back onto the highway.

Two hours into the trip, Rick suddenly heard an unusual noise under the hood and began smelling burning oil. He slowed down as the hearse filled with smoke. Before he could pull over, the engine blew. As had happened before, he was just coming up to a toll booth. Rick surmised that the unhappy mechanic had deliberately loosened the plug in the oil pan, allowing all the motor oil to gradually drain out, thus ruining the engine. As luck would have it, the toll booth operator was a very empathic fellow who had a friend who collected classic cars. He gave Rick the man's phone number, and Rick was able to get hold of him. The man quickly showed up at the toll plaza in a pink 1959 Desoto sedan and, after looking over the Packard, offered to swap the car for Rick's disabled hearse. That particular Desoto had an unpopular push-button shifting mechanism on the dash that had made it hard to sell, so he was happy to take the Packard in trade. Vehicular serendipity – one of the many blessings in Rick's life.

When Rick finally arrived on the Florida Southern College campus in his pink Desoto with his big bushy red hair and Coke bottle granny glasses, he soon ran afoul of the university's president, Charles Thrift, who was not amused by Rick's scruffy appearance. They knew each other from the year before when Rick had played many civic events at which the president had given speeches, often doing his rather outrageous folk-comedy routines. "I'm sure President Thrift was sick to death of hearing the sound of my voice, and when he saw my long-haired, hippie get up, that was it."

President Thrift sent word to Rick that his Methodist-sponsored college would not have anyone that looked like him on their campus and summarily dismissed him from the school. "That seemed a little strange to me," Rick recalled sarcastically, "as I'd been quite a popular and respected singer for the Methodist Church National Board of Evangelism all those years. Anyway, it was time to move on and, as I say, those experiences sure didn't get me religion, but it got me a lifetime of music."

Rick's musician friend, Knocky Parker, who had brought him aboard the Daytona *Caravan*, was a professor of English at the University of South Florida, just 35 miles away in Tampa. Rick called him, explained his predicament, and Knocky said he was sure he could get Rick into the sophomore class at USF. Rick packed up his things and headed to Tampa, arriving on the campus in the pink Desoto to a much warmer welcome.

Chapter Seven

WELCOME TO TAMPA

In the fall of 1966, thanks in large part to Knocky Parker's help, 21-year-old Rick Norcross soon felt quite at home at the University of South Florida. Situated on the north edge of Tampa, about ten miles from the center of the city, Rick described the area as "a small town backwater" compared to downtown Tampa. The school had a relatively small student population, and the music scene was quite off the beaten track compared to New York and London, where the folk scene had been so vibrant. While he continued to occasionally play as a solo artist, in the tradition of Harold Patch, Rick also started to pursue an interest in journalism, securing a job writing music reviews for the campus newspaper, *The Oracle*. Rick was appreciative that his father paid for his sophomore year's tuition, which enabled him to better concentrate on his studies.

Though there weren't a lot of places to hear or play music, there was one local bar, The Wild Boar, which offered some entertainment. It had been started by an English professor and sometimes hosted visiting writers and poets, including Jack Kerouac, who at that time lived in St. Petersburg. By the spring of 1967, Rick was convinced that the area needed a coffeehouse-type music venue that would feature folk singers as well as a variety of other entertainment. With his interest in music promotion growing, and having had a good experience with The Other Room in Lakeland, Rick was of a mind to put together a bigger, better showcase in Tampa. He wanted to offer "a bit of Bohemian Greenwich Village in the middle of a pretty square Florida."

To get things rolling, Rick reconnected with a friend he'd met in New York named Bill Utzig and convinced him to come down and partner on the new venture. Soon after Bill came onboard they found an open storefront close to the USF campus they could rent for $100 a month. In order for the coffeehouse to put up posters on campus, Rick had to get the school's Methodist Chapel Fellowship to sign on as a sponsor. In honor of his one-of-a-kind John Bailey guitar, Rick named his new haunt, The Eighteenth String Coffee House and Music Emporium.

Rick, Bill and a number of their college friends worked tirelessly to put the new coffeehouse together, including hanging colorful silkscreened paper eyeballs from the black ceiling. They decorated the club in a green and blue art nouveau style, complete with thick shag carpeting and plush cushions that lined the floor in front of the small stage. They brought in a disparate collection of furniture including a variety of miss-matched chairs as well as a set of old wooden church pews. Local artists were enlisted to exhibit their works on the walls, and Rick displayed a number of interesting antiques and curios he'd collected from local junk dealers, including a 1940's gumball machine. In addition to featured folk singers, the club planned to offer other types of entertainment on a regular schedule, including silent movies, tapes of classic old radio shows and a live Monday night open Hootenanny from nine to midnight. Rick even started an official newssheet called, *The Electric Lip*, which kept the area up to date with happenings at the club.

Rick knew that to get things off to a successful start he had to get the biggest name possible for the opening of their new coffeehouse. He contacted Carolyn Hester and was ecstatic when she agreed to headline opening night. By then Carolyn had released another successful album with Columbia Records and was much sought-after as a performer. It was testimony to their friendship and her respect for Rick as a musician and songwriter that she came through for him. On a Friday evening in early March 1967, Carolyn took the stage in front of a jam-packed house and The Eighteenth String was on its way.

Admission to the show was $1.50, and a simple menu of snacks and non-alcoholic beverages was served. Musicians and students from around the area came for the opening and the consensus was the night was a resounding success. During the following two years the club was in operation, Rick brought in a tremendous collection of both regional and national talent including Will McLean, Ramblin' Jack Elliot, Judy Roderick, Ed Freeman, and Gamble Rogers of the New Christy Minstrels.

Another singer who performed at the club was a fellow from St. Petersburg named Dan Finley, who later performed as "The Legendary Panama Red." Rick had met him while playing at the Beaux Arts club in Pinellas Park, Florida, and they had become friends. Panama Red played The Eighteenth String many times and went on to become the well known lead guitar player for Kinky Friedman and the Texas Jewboys. Rick remembered Panama Red as a spirited, versatile performer who he once witnessed do an amazing standing back flip on stage while playing a guitar solo! In turn, Panama Red considered Rick to have been a very special part of his musical journey. "After he opened The Eighteenth String, Rick Norcross was a pivotal character in my life as a musician and in the folk music scene in Tampa and St. Petersburg as well. He provided many of us with our first encounter with good folk music, bringing in acts I hadn't heard of yet but would later recognize as being prime members of the folk music pantheon like Vince Martin and Ramblin' Jack Elliot. But most importantly Rick provided a stage where a nervous young guy like me could begin to work on some sort of stage presence, play in front of people who listened and get paid. Not much, but *something*, some small token to give me the heart to continue this life of folly. Rick was also encouraging in that he learned a few songs I had written and actually performed them."

Many people who frequented The Eighteenth String in the 1960's have fondly reminisced about how important that very cool coffeehouse was, as it gave local young people a safe place to hang out amidst the turmoil of the Viet Nam War and escalating tensions over racial inequality and women's rights. One Tampa area singer who regularly performed at the club was Kathleen Gill. She and Rick lost touch with each other for over 40 years, but in 2010 Rick received an email from her in which she wrote, "I was greatly influenced by the Eighteenth String and it was *so* important during that period in my life. Playing there and listening to other artists ranks as one of the best times I've ever had in my life. So many great people passed through your doors. Thank you so much and I'm glad that you're well and still doing what you love all these years later." She was among dozens of musicians who have credited Rick with helping keep live music a vital part of the American arts scene.

After opening The Eighteenth String, to save money Rick moved into the back room of the coffeehouse and lived there for almost two years. "I was like a spider in my own web," he recalled, "and I loved it. There was so much going on — attending classes, writing for the school newspaper, performing and running the club — though by then my eyesight had gotten so bad I had a hard time recognizing people in the audience and feared I might go blind. Somehow I got to be seen at the Tampa Eye Clinic and the doctors were astounded at the severity of my steroid-induced cataracts. Despite being only in my early twenties, the only thing they could offer was to surgically remove the opacified cataracts from each eye to see if that would help my vision. I wasn't too excited about having someone cut into my eyeballs but I didn't *see* a good alternative either."

The arduous surgery and recovery took almost two years to complete, as each eye had to be patched for months after each procedure. Back then, surgeons were not able to implant artificial lenses to replace the diseased ones, so while Rick was finally free of the vision-clouding cataracts, he had no natural lenses left with which to focus. Therefore, he needed glasses to be able to see well.

Not one to let a little double eye surgery slow him down, Rick continued to perform solo, only he added a costume change to his act. "During those long months with a patched eye, I tried to accentuate the humor of the situation by mounting a stuffed parrot on the shoulder of my jacket and became known for doing some rather wild pirate songs along with my usual comedic folk routine. It made it easier for me, and luckily audiences loved it."

During that time, Rick met a fellow named Charles Fuller who owned a four-track recording studio in South Tampa. Rick remembered him as a "real nice guy" who had become successful doing voiceovers for commercials and promotional spots. At times Fuller leased his studio to bands, and in the fall of 1967, record producer Phil Gernhard rented Fuller's facility to record a record for a little known group from St. Petersburg called the Royal Guardsman. The song they recorded was "Snoopy vs. The Red Baron." Fortunately for Fuller, Gernhard didn't have enough money to pay for all the recording sessions up front, so he contracted with Fuller to pay him in part with points on profits from the recording if it was successful. And successful it was. Before long, it seemed like everyone in America and beyond was singing the catchy song and it soon rocketed to the top of the charts. Later, Gernhard became a very successful producer and promoter, bringing to the Tampa area top name acts including Elton John, Janis Joplin, B.B. King and Chuck Berry. Gernhard eventually went on to become a senior vice president of Curb Records in Nashville.

Charles Fuller did so well from his royalties he decided to branch out and become more involved with other aspects of the music business. At that time, The Eighteenth String was the hottest music scene around, so Fuller approached Rick and his partner about buying in as a part owner. They struck a deal, and Fuller invested some of his own money in the club, installing recording equipment (with Rick's permission) so that he could make recordings of artists' performances. Fuller was also interested in recording some of Rick's songs and signed him to record an album in his studio. To help with the record, Rick contacted a musician and arranger from Boston he had previously met named,

Ed Freeman, and brought him to Tampa to produce the album and to perform at the club. Rick's friend, Knocky Parker also came into the studio to play ragtime piano on one of the album's songs, "The Abyssinian Desert Monkey Rag."

Despite their best efforts, Rick's album didn't turn out as well as they'd hoped, so it didn't get released. Fuller was able to release a couple of 45's of cover material including a song by Fred Neil called, "Searching for the Dolphins." The singles got a fair amount of airplay in Florida and in Vermont, but didn't really take off beyond that. While Rick was glad to finally have something on vinyl, he had not been able to record and release his own material, which remained his goal, though perhaps against long odds. He realized the strength of his own songs was strongly tied to live audience participation and that his early attempts at recording weren't translating into records that were good to just sit and listen to. It was also the first time Freeman had produced a folk record and Rick says he worked very hard on the project. "Even though it wasn't successful, it seemed Freeman got enough enjoyment out of producing my record that he became interested in pursuing a career as a producer. He went on to become a renowned producer of many successful records including Don McLean's megahit, 'American Pie,' and all of Tom Rush's Columbia albums."

Later that year, Rick heard from Diz Disley, who was in Canada visiting his birthplace. Rick invited Diz to come to Tampa to play at The Eighteenth String and to meet his new partner, Charles Fuller, who was familiar with Diz's outstanding musicianship and outrageous exploits in England. Fuller came to the club and saw Diz perform and was so impressed he offered him a contract to record at his studio.

Diz performed in Tampa for about two months while living on a couch at The Eighteenth String. He worked on some recordings with Fuller and Rick also recorded some of Diz's comedic folk material at the club. However, as Rick recalled, "These were *not* the accommodations Diz was accustomed to and he was not a happy camper, to say the least. My music circles and living arrangements were way lower than he was used to in England and though people

86

enjoyed him, by his standards the audiences were very small. I think that was terribly embarrassing for him so he soon lost interest in playing in Florida, and couldn't wait to get out of here. Unfortunately, Diz was even worse than I was for hanging onto money — and he actually *had* some — so he ended up having to sell one of his guitars to raise enough money to get back to England. Pretty shabby for the guy who had driven me around London in a Rolls Royce meeting his celebrity friends just two years before."

Though Diz may have thought otherwise, Rick felt that he and Fuller had done everything they could to promote his shows, but it just hadn't worked out. As soon as he had enough money for a plane ticket, Diz left for England in a huff and that's when things got ugly. Rick again took some time off from school and through his London agency, was booked into a busy performance schedule in England for April and May of 1968. Rick recalled, "Little did I know when Diz arrived back in London he told my agent that I had decided to cancel my upcoming British tour and that I was going to stay in the States. The English clubs I was supposed to play for were extremely disappointed and angry and had to scramble to fill my tour dates. Trying to *help out*, Diz proceeded to take all my bookings for himself."

Back in Florida, Rick was excited as he made preparations to return to England where he'd had such a great experience during his '65-'66 stay. He had no idea that Diz had undermined him until he stepped off the plane at Heathrow Airport and found a couple of unfriendly immigration officers waiting for him. "Not only had Diz stolen my tour dates, I found out he'd also alerted the authorities that an undocumented American folk singer named Rick Norcross would be trying to sneak into the country and even supplied them with my flight number!"

"I was dumbfounded — just couldn't believe Diz could go that low. I'd heard stories about underhanded stuff he'd pulled on others, but this was unbelievable." True to form, however, Rick took a breath, asked the authorities to step aside with him for a few minutes and in his friendliest, most persuasive

East Hardwick dialect, explained to them it was all a misunderstanding. He convinced them he was there to "conduct cultural research on the wonderful English people" so that he could write new songs about them. Rick chuckles when he looked back on that very close call. "I lied through my teeth, they bought it, and I hit the road to London."

Once back in his old haunts, he quickly reconnected with Derek Sarjeant, and when he and others found out what Diz had done, they bent over backwards to book Rick into a good folk club schedule for the six weeks he was there, including back at the Assembly Rooms in Surbiton.

Rick never palled around with Diz again. Leaving his comedic folk music behind, Diz went on to become a world-renown jazz guitarist who, in 1972, thrilled the music world by coaxing Django Reinhardt's original partner, the great jazz violinist Stephane Grappelli, out of retirement to play with him. For the next ten years they toured the world from Carnegie Hall to the great concert halls of Europe and Australia. As Rick said, "Diz ended up making a small fortune from his new collaborations and his life certainly became a far cry from sleeping on a couch in the back of The Eighteenth String."

As the years wore on, however, Diz's excessive drinking eventually caught up with him and his health started to fail. He reportedly was fond of proclaiming the following regarding his alcohol intake: "I always carry brandy in case I am bitten by a snake, which I also carry;" and "I only drink to steady myself and sometimes I get so steady, I can't move." He eventually suffered a heart attack and developed a form of dementia that deprived him of his musical genius.

Rick reminisced about those days. "Unfortunately, Diz, like so many high-flying artists, and despite his remarkable resurgence, still ended up having a sad ending to his life. There was just something about him, that no matter how much fame and fortune he attained, as someone once said, he had a 'built in anti-success mechanism.' I felt very sad when I later learned that toward the end Diz became unable to even play his guitar and died alone and penniless in a small flat in London."

Back in the States, Rick spent much of his time at The Eighteenth String, where many local students came to enjoy music. One night he met a beautiful young woman named Beverly, who had just graduated from college and was teaching in Tampa. They both loved music, hung out together at the club and eventually started dating. Rick recalled, "Beverly was a great gal who was a lot of fun and I also really liked her family and enjoyed being around them. Her father was a very hard working guy who owned a large cement company, and – very importantly – her mother was a great cook."

It was exceptionally hot in Tampa that summer and Rick longed to get back to the cooler mountains of Vermont. Just as he'd dreamed of palm trees during the brutally cold winters of his childhood, the fresh air and simpler life of East Hardwick beckoned and he had a special girl he wanted to bring home to show his native State to. Also, as much as he'd enjoyed all the excitement and success of The Eighteenth String, he was ready to get back out on the road and focus on his own performing. That summer he was able to get some good gigs up north opening for national acts, as well as a spot playing at the *Cape Cod Music Festival* in Falmouth, MA, with acts such as Dick Creeden's Village Green Dixies, and Linda James and The Sheparoos.

Despite its popularity, The Eighteenth String eventually became less fun and more of a burden. Rick and the other owners had to constantly scrounge around to keep the schedule filled and to make enough money to support the operation of the club. By late 1968, to the disappointment of hundreds of loyal patrons, the club closed its doors after celebrating with several nights of great performances. At that point, Rick needed to make money and was able to get a job at the Slack Shack, a local boutique pants store. As he liked to say, "I was a crack Slack Shack slack stacker stacking Slack Shack slacks! And working there allowed me to buy some fairly outrageous clothing, including my favorite outfit which consisted of a blue blazer, orange tie and white bellbottoms."

By October 1969, still slowly working his way through college as he could afford it, Rick saw an interesting ad for a new position at the *Tampa Times*, the city's afternoon newspaper. The job entailed writing a music and arts column for a special section called "ETC," which would be devoted to attracting more readership from the youth in the Tampa Bay area. Filled with bravado and chutzpah, Rick strode into the *Times* building, boisterously made his way past the reporters working the newsroom, to the office of legendary editor, H. Doyle Harvill. Harvill was known to be a very sharp journalist, a tough contrarian who seemed intrigued by this self-promoting young Norcross fellow. To his staff's surprise, Harvill ended up hiring Rick for the paper's new section.

Rick shook his head as he recalled, "I was dressed in my new, rather loud outfit and I'm sure Mr. Harvill's staff thought he would literally throw me out of his office. Luckily for me, Harvill heard two of his editors laughing at me as I headed into his office and I'm sure he hired me just to shock those guys. In reality, my experiences playing so much in England and the fact that I owned the popular Eighteenth String, led Mr. Harvill to respect me enough to hire me. By then, I had also been the Fine Arts Editor of the University of South Florida's newspaper and that lent me additional credibility. And the truth is, for the next five years I worked very hard for that newspaper and it paid off for both of us."

Rick's friend, Frank Ross, had just gotten home from his military duties in Southeast Asia and was hired as a photographer at the *Times'* sister paper, the *Tampa Tribune*. At one of his first official meetings between the papers, Frank was surprised and delighted when Rick, whom he'd respected as owner of The Other Room in Lakeland in 1964, was introduced as the new entertainment writer at the *Times*.

Frank reminisced, "That period in the newspaper business was interesting for sure as they were always looking for talented, enthusiastic young people to exploit and Rick and I were ripe for the picking. Management was aware that Rick was a walking encyclopedia about the music scene and that his reviews in the college paper were very insightful, so they were smart to hire him. Newspapers were just starting to make the transition from pretty stark layouts of sterile columns and occasional posed *mug shots*, to layouts using much more dramatic images that dominated the page. Besides music, photography was another area where Rick and I shared a common passion. He was very bright and looked at assignments as exciting opportunities to photograph entertainers, often in concert settings and bring the excitement of live performances to the page. He really understood the importance of images to illustrate his articles and lobbied the editors hard to use his photographs prominently and they did. Rick really knew what he was doing and those illustrated articles —which we now take for granted — drew more attention to his work and the exposure was good for a young photographer and writer who also happened to be a very talented musician. In addition to having a fine finesse on a guitar or banjo, he was also a great word smith."

Frank had some very advanced Canon camera gear that he had bought in Japan on his way home from Viet Nam. Other *Tribune* photographers chided him for not using the industry standard Nikon cameras, so he sold his Canon gear to Rick at a great price. This allowed Rick to augment his music reviews with stunning candid photographs that he took only in the available light in concert halls, without the use of the large *exploding* flashbulbs of the day. As Rick, the new *Tampa Times* Entertainment Editor was about to find out, he was poised to step into the big time.

Rick (8th from left) with his Mother and Father on the *Ticonderoga* during its last voyage,
Nov. 6, 1954

Rick learning to play first guitar in Harold Patch's living room,
East Hardwick, Vermont, 1961.

Neighbor Harold Patch painting his home, East Hardwick 1971.

Rick and classmate, Alberta Kinny, at Hardwick Academy Class Day, 1963.

The New Walden Folk Singers, Cypress Gardens, Florida, Fall 1963:
Rick (left), Tom Azarian (center), Bud Boydston.

Rick and friends recording at Casswin Studio, Lakeland, FL, 1963

1934 GMC Rick salvaged from Bud Boydston's Walden, Vermont pasture, 1964.

Rick's 1933 International pick 'em up truck he swapped for a nice Plymouth, 1964.

1960's publicity photo for The Eighteenth String, Tampa, Florida

Rick's 1937 Packard hearse at Perkin's Pier, Burlington, Vermont waterfront.

Rick and Kayle Payne performing at the Other Room
Coffee House, Lakeland, FL.,1964.

Bob Dylan and Pete Seeger on stage at the *Newport Folk Festival*, July 1964.

Rick with his unique 18 String Guitar, London City Agency publicity photo, 1965.

Rick performing with British folk group, The Natterjacks, England, 1965.

THE ASSEMBLY ROOMS • SURBITON, ENGLAND

Rear, Left to Right, Derek Sarjeant, Diz Disley, Johnny Parker, Peggy Phango, Laurie Chescoe, Sugar Bill Robinson. Front, Rick Norcross

From 1965 to 1975, Rick Norcross toured England extensively performing as a solo artiste in clubs, universities, festivals and on BBC Radio and Television. Derek Sarjeant's Assembly Rooms in Surbiton, South London, was one of Britain's largest and most popular music clubs and one of Rick's favorite haunts. This photo was taken following a rousing performance with a group of England's top jazz musicians on January 19, 1966.

Promotional broadside from concert at Assembly Rooms, Surbiton, England 1966.

RICK NORCROSS

Rick performing in British band jacket, University of South Florida, Tampa, FL., 1966.

Coffee House Opening
To Star Carolyn Hester

By POLLY WEAVER
Feature Editor

The eighteenth string is one too many for most guitar players, but The Eighteenth String coffee house seems to be playing it cool and agile, judging by the talent line-up scheduled for its grand opening Friday.

Rick Norcross, owner and folksinger in his own right, announced that Carolyn Hester, nationally famous folksinger, will appear at the first show.

United Artist writer Jerry Merrick will perform second and Allan Stowell and Kurt Anderson from Orlando third. Stowell and Anderson are old-time bluegrass singers.

Show time is 7:45 p.m. Friday and Saturday at 10,622 30th St. next to the University Exchange Bookstore. Admission is $1.50.

Paintings by Jeff Dunn, SAR and area art award winners will be exhibited. There will be a folksing Sunday from 9 p.m. to midnight.

The decor will be in blue and green "art nouveau" style.

CAROLYN HESTER
... to appear Friday

Huge carpeting and cushions will line the floor in front of the stage with church pews in the rear. One of the unusual accessories is a gum ball machine.

Inexpensive drinks will be served, but no alcoholic beverages.

The coffee house has no connection with the University, although it has received help in becoming established from the Chapel Fellowship; faculty members including Mesrop Kesdekian, artist-in-residence this trimester, and several students.

Annual memberships may be available later according to Norcross. The memberships will lower the price for most activities.

Each night will be devoted to a special activity ranging in price from 50 to 75 cents on week nights.

The tentative schedule is for silent movies on Wednesday night and discussions on Sunday. Other evenings will in-

RICK NORCROSS
... to provide song

clude drama, jazz, old radio tapes and others.

Carolyn Hester has several LP's out, including "Carolyn Hester at Town Hall 1 and 2" and "That's My Song."

She has made tours of England and has appeared on the "Tonight Show," "Merv Griffin Show" and at The Bitter End and The Gaslight in New York. Bob Dylan was discovered playing harmonica backups on one of Miss Hester's records.

Norcross was a student at USF last trimester and plans to continue next trimester. He toured England, appearing in various folk clubs, cabarets and at the Cambridge and Stevenage Folk Festivals.

Returning to the U.S., he played engagements on the East Coast, including Club 47 in Boston, The Gaslight, The Bitter End.

He accompanies himself on the guitar, banjo, auto-harp, harmonica and a special 18-string guitar he had custom made by John Bailey of London.

Norcross issued a plea for students to bring pop-top tops ("soft drinks of course") for use in making chains.

Student Pay De
Present Tax Pro

By ERNA SCHERFFIUS
Correspondent

Income tax and social security payroll deductions are a fact of life for most of the working world. For the working student these two deductions can present some problems.

There are approximately 700 students working part time at USF, according to Louis R. Cacciatore, supervising accountant for the Division of Finance & Accounting. Last December, there were 714 students with a total payroll of $49,398.

NO SOCIAL security deductions are taken from these earnings in accordance with State Comptroller's Regulations. A contract between the U.S. Government and USF exempts the University from making the social security deductions. Non - profit organi-

zations may enter into such contracts.

NO SUCH contract is possible for income tax deductions. This deduction is made on a percentage method based on the exemptions claimed on the W-4 form, "Employee's Withholding Exemption Certificate," that each employee must file with his employer. The percentage method uses tables furnished by the Internal Revenue Service and broken down as to number of exemptions claimed, total earnings and the payroll period (hourly, weekly, monthly, etc.). These percentages do not apply unless the employee earns over $900, and if he claims one exemption.

IF INSUFFICIENT deductions for income tax purposes have been made, it very often occurs when one has had multiple employers during the year and claims a personal

Football Committee

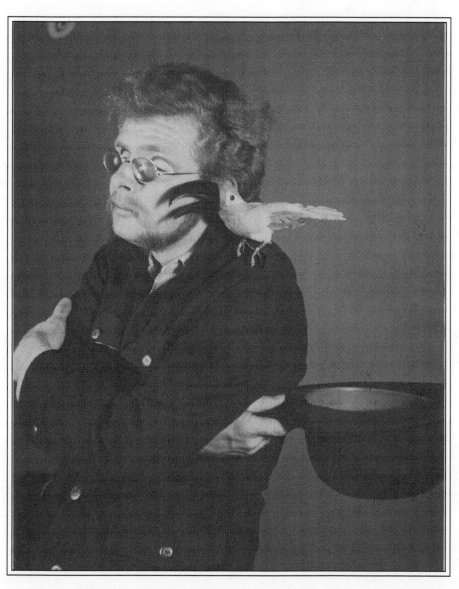

Rick performing with parrot sidekick after cataract surgery at age 22, 1967.

Rick working backstage for *Tampa Times* at Allman Brothers concert,
Tampa Stadium 1973.

Janis Joplin performing at Curtis-Hixon Hall,
Tampa, FL, the night she was arrested, 1970.

Elvis making them swoon at Curtis-Hixon Hall, Tampa, FL., 1970.

One of Rick's rare candid photos of Elvis at Curtis-Hixon Hall, Tampa, FL., 1970

Rick's *Tampa Times* photo of Johnny Cash and June Carter Cash, Lakeland, FL., 1973

Rick's *Tampa Times* photo of Bob Dylan performing with the Band, Hollywood, FL., 1974.

Rick and Pete Yorkunas in London during British folk tour, 1974.

Rick on the porch of his home, El Rancho Tedioso, Ybor City, Tampa, FL, 1974.

Promotional photo of Rick on Church Street, Burlington,
Vermont with 1952 Nash Rambler, 1976.

Rick at the Florida State Fair with the Ink Spots, 1982.

Rick in front of Flynn Theater before show with Hank Williams' Drifting Cowboys, Burlington, Vermont 1980.

Rick and close friend, Dan Dubonnet, at his WOKO studios, 2013.

Promotional photo of Rick on 1959 Rambler at El Rancho Tedioso, Tampa, FL, 1980's.

Rick's *Tour de Jour* album cover shoot at Rambler Ranch, Burlington, Vermont 1985

Larry, his brother, Darryl, and his other brother, Darryl, from CBS's *Newhart Show* at the *Chew Chew Festival*, Burlington, Vermont, 1984.

Rick and Rockabilly singer, Rosie Flores at the *Chew Chew Festival*, Burlington, Vermont, 1994.

Barb "P-Bear" Bardin working the *Chew Chew Festival*, Bennington, Vermont 1995.

Rick and the Ramblers in front of the *Pickle* at Lake St. Catherine State Park show, 2010.

Rick (The Tampa Chicken) and radio personality, Jack Donovan,
at WDEV's 55th anniversary party, Middlesex, Vermont, 1984.

Miranda Lambert visiting the *Pickle* backstage at the WOKO *Country Club Music Festival,* Essex, Vermont 2005.

Rick and U.S. Senator Pat Leahy on the *Pickle*. Photo by Marcelle Leahy.

Rick in front of beloved *Ticonderoga* steamboat, Shelburne Museum 2010. (James Teuscher, Photo)

Ramblers playing *Vermont Day*, Big E, Springfield, MA, 2009:

Ken Grillo, Doug Reid, Buck Maynard, Dave Rowell, Rick Norcross, Julia Shannon-Grillo, Charlie MacFadyen, Josie Ritter, and Brett Hoffman.

Rambler songstress, Taryn Noelle, performing with the band, Burlington, Vermont 2008.

Rick performing with drummer Genis Ferri Navarro in Murcia, Spain, 2010.

Frank Ross and Rick at UU Dome Concert, Tampa, FL., March 2011.

LeRoy Preston and Julia Shannon-Grillo at the *Pickle Party*, Burlington, Vermont, March 2012.

Bear Bessette in front of the *Pickle* being restored in his Hardwick, Vermont shop 2012.

Ken Grillo, Julia Shannon-Grillo, and Joan Shannon, Burlington, Vermont 2012.

Ramblers performing at Burlington's Perkins Pier before fireworks 2012.

Rick trying (unsuccessfully) to teach Steve to sing at Rambler Ranch, Jan. 2013.
Photo by Natalie Stultz.

The Ramblers performing at Farmers' Night, Vermont State House 2013: Buck Maynard, Rick, Taryn Noelle, Dave Rowell, Julia Shannon-Grillo. Photo by Andy Duback.

Chapter Eight

BB & JANIS

Rick's first music assignment for the *Times* was a major concert at Tampa's largest venue, Curtis Hixon Hall. The headliner was "America's first girl rock star," Janis Joplin. And what a night it was. When Rick arrived with his brand new press pass, he made his way to his front row seat as a crowd of over 3500 jammed into the auditorium. The mostly young audience was seething with energy, anxiously awaiting the appearance of arguably the most famous female rock singer in the world. Warming up the crowd, Sonny Freeman and the Originals played then legendary bluesman, B. B. King took the stage. Rick recalled, "King was cool as a cucumber, a top-notch professional who took command of the show from the moment he stepped on stage through *four* standing ovations. I still remember the final strains from his faithful guitar, Lucille, dissipating into the night. The audience was with him the whole time, including as he left the stage flashing a peace sign and his trademark wide grin."

After an equipment change and backed by a great band, which included a full brass section and an organ, Janis Joplin took the stage, her long hair tangled about her face, her forearms ringed with colorful bangle bracelets. She grabbed hold of the microphone and belted out an opening song, immediately followed by her super hit, "Piece of My Heart." That was when much of the adoring audience came unglued. In the 1960's, concert decorum called for the audience to stay in their seats during shows so the entire crowd could clearly see the performers on the stage. But that night, despite the best efforts of several Tampa police officers to control them, things got pretty crazy.

Rick clearly remembered that night, "At that point, 500 kids suddenly surged to the front of the stage in an effort to get closer to the superstar. As the police tried to move the crowd back to their seats, Joplin yelled at the cops, 'Get out of my show!' Unfortunately, things rapidly deteriorated and the other 3000 paying fans weren't able to see the stage. After another song, Joplin yelled to the crowd, 'If you want to see, stand on a chair!' and that's exactly what they did. Clearly, Tampa wasn't ready for a Janis Joplin-style rock and roll performance, which soon turned to chaos."

The next morning, Rick reported in his review, "At one point in Joplin's program the authorities turned off her mikes and turned up the house lights in an attempt to restrain the crowd. But nothing worked and in the end, Miss Joplin only did seven songs which was a disappointment to all her fans that came to hear her music as opposed to a marathon audience rush."

As soon as the short-lived concert ended, Rick hurried backstage to Joplin's dressing room and interviewed her about what had happened. A few minutes later, several Tampa police officers barged in and arrested her on two counts of using indecent language in public, alleging that she swore at the police during the show. Her widely publicized arrest that night was featured in newspapers around the world, many of which ran photos taken by Rick.

Early the next morning, Rick went down to police headquarters where Joplin was being held to talk with her before her arraignment. After the proceedings, as much as he liked her music, it was clear to Rick that Joplin had acted irresponsibly and had a big hand in what had gone on the night before, antagonizing both the police and the audience, which she repeatedly urged to rush the stage. Rick wrote about it in a follow up piece in the *Times* a few days later, titled, "Joplin Hurt the Music Scene." He aptly pointed out that "nobody was corrupted in hearing a couple of indecent words that we all had heard before anyway. The real issue was the damage done to the local music scene itself." He had the journalistic guts and musical devotion to end the piece with, "Janis Joplin owes Tampa an apology."

What the public discovered in Rick's first professional music review was a reporter who set a high standard for himself, and for the Tampa music scene. Already a highly-respected performer and former coffeehouse owner, Rick soon gained the additional respect and following of thousands of *Tampa Times* readers through his honest and insightful journalism.

A year later Janis Joplin died of a heroin overdose at the age of 27 and one of Rick's candid photos of her from that fateful night in Tampa appeared on the covers of newspapers and magazines worldwide. It was the first of many up front, painful examples of how drugs and alcohol tragically claimed the lives of so many of his fellow artists, and a warning to him – in sync with his grand-mother Delilah's admonitions – that he'd better "watch his step."

Rick appreciated the talented staff he worked with at the *Times*, including a woman named, Abby Kaighin. "Abby was a terrific friend and a very, very sharp reporter. I always had huge respect for her, and especially appreciated the way she covered difficult stories, like some of the race riots in Tampa."

Abby laughed when she remembered working at the *Times* with Rick. "In Tampa, Rick was simply amazing. Even his clothes made everyone take note. It was the era of bell bottoms but Rick took it to a whole different level. Our newsroom was crazy; we all worked for close to nothing but had such fun. It was like a big family of kids led by a wiser, older, more experienced editor, Doyle Harvill. Can you imagine this costumed music critic from the hills of Vermont somehow getting the Korean War vet, hard-nosed editor to go to the Atlanta Rock Festival?"

Rick remembered well when he and Mr. Harvill covered that festival together. "It was the *huge* rock festival in Atlanta. I was set to go and Harvill came rolling out of his office and informed me he was coming along with me.

We ended up camping out in a tent and really covered that important festival. He wrote an editorial about the scene and I wrote about the music. I still remember how much fun it was driving up I-75 in his Ford LTD mixing rum drinks, instead of my heading north alone in my little Pinto."

During the time Rick and Abby worked together at the *Times*, her husband was an Air Force fighter pilot stationed in Viet Nam. When he finished that tour of duty, he was transferred to the Royal Air Force base in Woodbridge, England, and Abby moved there to be with him. When Rick returned for another folk tour in England in 1974, he reconnected with Abby, visiting her on the air base where her husband was stationed. She recalled Rick driving up from London in a big car called a Humber Super Snipe, which she said had very little in the way of brakes. They had many great times during Rick's visits and she particularly remembered that "he was a fabulous cook," making "the best guacamole I'd ever had."

During that tour of England, when Rick was playing the Troubadour Club in London, Abby, her husband and a group of friends from the air base would come down to see him perform and great times were had by all.

Over his five years at the *Times*, Rick interviewed and photographed every major musical act that came to the Tampa area, which had become a major American concert stop. At most shows, he was able to spend time on stage and backstage with the superstars of the day, including the Rolling Stones, Led Zeppelin, Eric Clapton and Derrick and the Dominoes, Crosby, Stills, Nash and Young, Blood, Sweat and Tears, The Byrds, Vanilla Fudge, Johnny Winter, and his old friend from his London days, Donovan. He also hung out with many country stars, including Johnny Cash, Merle Haggard and George Jones. During those years, Rick had some remarkable experiences, not just interviewing and photographing artists, but also learning the ropes of major event production and what made certain events more successful than others. This accumulated knowledge proved invaluable later in his career when he returned to Vermont and became a successful event producer in his own right.

One experience that stood out in Rick's memory was a night he covered Jerry Garcia and the Grateful Dead at a sold out show at Tampa's Curtis Hixon Hall. After the show Rick photographed and talked with the band backstage until Garcia called it a night and left. Rick left shortly thereafter and when he walked out the back door of the hall, to his surprise he found a very frustrated Garcia pacing back and forth on the loading dock waiting for his limousine. Showing the star a little Yankee hospitality, Rick offered to give Garcia a ride back to his hotel and he didn't hesitate to accept. Rick ran and got his Ford Pinto woody wagon, threw as much of his debris in the back as he could, dusted off the passenger's seat, then drove over and picked up Garcia. Rick thought it was pretty cool riding around Tampa with the Dead's front man sitting next to him and was relieved the Pinto was actually firing on all four of its cylinders.

Other experiences Rick remembered included a night when he hung out and drank good whiskey with Boots Randolph, Floyd Cramer, and Chet Atkins. Another night he watched what to Rick looked like a high-stakes poker game in a hotel room with Charlie Pride and other performers after a show. The pinnacle of his five year run at the *Times*, however, was the night in 1970 he covered Elvis, when he came out of early retirement and dazzled 14,000 wildly cheering fans at Curtis Hixon. The rare photographs Rick took of Elvis that night are arguably some of the best candid shots ever taken of the King and are collector's items today. Through hard work and a keen artistic eye, Rick Norcross established himself as one of the finest music photographers around.

During the late Sixties and early Seventies, alcohol and drugs took down many great talents, including Rick's friend, Gram Parsons, who had become very influential in bringing about the successful blending of country and rock music. After Parson's early solo career when he and Rick had met, Parsons went on to an illustrious singing career. He became a member of the Byrds in 1968 after David Crosby left, and was instrumental in putting together their highly-respected album, *Sweetheart of the Rodeo.* Parsons went on to sing in The Flying Burrito Brothers, followed by a recording collaboration with Emmylou Harris.

By then, Gram had descended into serious alcohol and drug addiction, which limited his creativity and threatened his health. After his home burned to the ground in the summer of 1973, Parsons spent much of his time tripping on LSD in the desert area of Joshua Tree, California, where he died in a cinderblock motel of an overdose at the age of 26. Having known Parsons personally, and realizing his huge creative potential, Rick was saddened and frightened by the news of his death. "Great artists were dropping like flies back then and I took notice."

The year 1971 brought the unthinkable — marriage. Coming from a dysfunctional family, Rick approached matrimony with great trepidation, but Beverly had taken hold and they ended up getting married in Tampa. Her parents held an elegant reception at the exclusive Tampa Yacht and Country Club and to his bride's relief, Rick did not wear the British band coat with the attached parrot. Wanting someone from Vermont to be there, and even though he'd had little contact with her, Rick asked his mother to fly down for the wedding. Not surprisingly, she declined, her excuse being her deep-seated fear of flying, a result of her terrifying experience flying over the Bristol, Vermont cemetery with his father at the controls in the late 1940's. Sadly for Rick, not a single Vermonter was at his nuptials.

In juxtaposition to the fancy wedding, Rick and Beverly headed north for a honeymoon at his family's house in East Hardwick, where they enjoyed that wonderful feather bed. That was, until Beverly's mother and sister arrived for an unexpected visit. Grammy Delilah had passed away by the time Rick married, but when he and Beverly arrived, Rick found his dear friend and mentor, Harold Patch — then in his mid eighties — up on a ladder painting his house. Unable to bear the thought of Mr. Patch falling, Rick took over and spent a good share of his honeymoon painting the rest of the house, for which Patch gave him the last kitchen clock he had personally salvaged from the mountains of tangled debris jamming the Waterbury, Vermont dam after the devastating 1927 flood. That fall, tremendous rains had ravaged north central Vermont, killing 84 people including Lt. Governor Hollister Jackson. Countless homes and businesses were destroyed as raging flood waters took out an astonishing 1285 bridges.

Though Rick had continued to visit Vermont during college vacations, his honeymoon trip poignantly reminded him of how much he missed the verdant hills and valleys of the Northeast Kingdom. While there, he learned that the local paper, *The Hardwick Gazette,* was for sale and with his serious interest in journalism, he considered buying it. He thought that he and Beverly could move up from Florida and he would become the editor of the paper and Beverly would teach school. To help him make a decision, Rick asked *Tampa Times* Editor Doyle Harvill to come to Hardwick to review the newspaper's books and see if he thought the paper was a reasonable investment.

Mr. Harvill was kind enough to fly up to look at the *Gazette's* ledgers and he liked what he saw. Rick and two others put in a bid to buy the *Gazette* but in the end another local journalist purchased the paper and hired Rick as the editor. Beverly headed back to her graduate studies in Florida and Rick took over as editor of his old hometown paper. Unfortunately, the new owner did not pay his bills or Rick in a timely fashion, therefore the whole arrangement soon fell apart. The new owner lost the paper and Rick lost his editor's job.

Realizing things were not going to work in Hardwick, Rick headed back to Tampa, where worse news awaited him. During the time he was in Hardwick trying to make a go of the *Gazette,* his new wife had turned her attentions elsewhere and lost interest in their marriage. Rick was very upset by the situation, and it was clear there would be no reconciliation, so he and his wife divorced in 1972. Though the divorce took a painful toll, he looked back on it with his typical wry humor. "That was a very stressful year during which I lost 140 pounds: 100 for Beverly and 40 for me!" That was also the year Rick finally finished his ten-year college education, graduating from the University of South Florida with a degree in journalism.

Rick had left the *Tampa Times* to become the editor of the *Hardwick Gazette*, but when that plan fell through, he got back in touch with Mr. Harvill, who agreed to hire him back on at the newspaper. Rick sold his family's home in East Hardwick and bought a house in an old Tampa neighborhood called Ybor City, center of the once flourishing cigar industry. Rick named his nondescript new home "El Rancho Tedioso."

The vibrant, Cuban-influenced culture of Tampa's old neighborhoods drew Rick in, including the large brick edifices that were once humming cigar factories. Now closed down, those factories belied a once vibrant industry that was a foundation of Tampa's early development. In fact, it was in the early 1900's that a Spaniard named Don Vicente de Ybor began moving most of the existing cigar factories from Key West to the downtown Tampa neighborhood which was later named Ybor City. Eventually Tampa became the center of cigar making in America and took on the nickname "Cigar City." In its heyday, Tampa had over 30 factories working long shifts producing cigars with American tobacco covered with special Cuban wrapper leaves.

Ybor City was known in the mid 1950's for visits from an increasingly powerful Cuban named Fidel Castro. He would fly over from Havana and hold court in a well known Spanish restaurant, The Columbia, which had been established in 1905. Walking the streets on a Saturday night, Rick enjoyed the rich, warm aromas of Cuban dishes wafting from the cafes: saffron and adobo, black beans, yellow rice and hot sauce, Boliche Cubano, and Ropa Vieja. He also liked to listen to the animated repartee of Cubans on the streets and in the bars.

One of Rick's new neighbors in Ybor City was a wonderful fellow in his eighties named Joe Fernandez, who everyone called "Mr. Pepine," which meant grandfather. As they became friends, Rick loved listening to Joe's stories about the early days in Ybor City when he worked as the maitre d' at the Columbia. Mr. Pepine related to Rick that during 1958 the Columbia hosted Fidel Castro for lunch every day for six months while he was temporarily living in the area. Castro met with expatriate locals to raise money for his forthcoming Revolution, which finally ousted the previous dictator, Batista, in 1959. Castro was quite famous and insisted someone from the restaurant staff sit with him during lunch to fend off anyone that would approach him that he didn't want to talk to. Mr. Pepine was given the special task of spending every lunch time sitting across from Castro at his private table, constantly keeping an eye on who was in the restaurant and running interference when necessary. Apparently he got many earfuls of Castro's legendary ranting and raving and described him to Rick in one succinct and telling word, "Coo-coo," while making circular motions above his head.

In the 1970's, Rick continued to play as a headliner during the winter at Florida venues including Beaux Arts, Clancy's Irish Pub in St. Petersburg, Tomfoolery in Tampa, and at the *Palm Beach* and *Florida Folk Festivals*. He also kept busy interviewing artists that came to town and one in particular brought him some good fortune. Tommy Overstreet was a successful singer from Nashville, who had charted three number one singles. When he came to play Tampa, Rick decided to write a story about him. While Rick was interviewing Overstreet, he took out a new, partially written song and sang it for Rick, telling him that he was having a hard time finishing the lyrics. That night Rick went home and pulled out one of his own half-written songs and used those lyrics to complete Overstreet's song. The next day when Rick sang the completed song for Overstreet, he loved it and ended up recording it on ABC Records.

The song was "Sleep My Lady, Dream of Me," and when the album went to the top of the Billboard charts, reviewers positively mentioned that song in particular, which eventually rose to number 19 on the country charts. Rick received credit on the album for his contribution to the song and began receiving royalty checks from Overstreet's publisher, Circle T Music Company. Rick recalled, "The success of that one song with Tommy Overstreet was exciting and I thought I would soon be making serious money on my songwriting, so I got cocky."

By 1974, Rick decided to leave the newspaper business and turn his full attention to his first loves of writing, playing and producing music. After he left the paper, however, Rick did not have other songwriting successes as substantial as he'd had with Overstreet. Fortunately, his old friend Frank Ross had also moved on from the newspaper business and gone to work at the *Florida State Fair*, which featured some of the biggest shows in the area each year. When Frank was promoted to the position of executive director, he turned to Rick and asked him to come on board as manager of The Sunshine Theater, one of the fair's largest and most important venues.

Frank recalled, "This large theater seated over 2000 people and had a non-stop flow of all types of entertainment. Rick's job was to keep all the acts happy, getting them teed up, on and off stage at the right times, and handling the professional introductions as well. It was an extremely demanding job and it was a real comfort for me to know that Rick was taking care of this very important theater and he handled it flawlessly. And part of the reason he was able to handle it so well is that Rick always has a smile on his face and never met a musician or entertainer he didn't like; or a person for that matter. This collection of traits has served him well over the years in so many capacities and makes me real proud to call Rick Norcross my good friend. As so many other people near and far have experienced, knowing him for over 40 years has been a blessing in many ways."

Working at the *Florida State Fair* gave Rick valuable experience in producing large scale events. It also allowed him to make enough money to support his own singing career on the side, usually performing solo or with a talented female vocalist named Nancy Cox Johnson. Rick also played larger shows, like the fair, for which he put together a four-piece band with some of his friends who were local session musicians.

During 1974, Rick returned to England for another tour of the folk clubs he had enjoyed so much during the 1960's. By then his 18 string guitar had worn out and he was performing with a top-of-the-line Martin D-45, which had inlaid abalone edges and a unique black lacquer face. One night Rick's guitar was stolen after playing the Troubadour Club in London. "After the show I was invited to a party at a nearby flat and like a fool, left the D-45 in the car on the street. When I came out, the guitar was gone. That was a real blow as it was a very special guitar and I felt very badly about it. After that major setback, I never returned to England to play."

Once Rick was back home, he contacted a former Martin Company luthier, Paul Buskirk, who built him what came to be known as the "Wonder Guitar," a replacement D-45 with aged wood Buskirk had bought during his days working at Martin. Rick commissioned a custom inlaid Tree of Life on the fingerboard, and again had the face lacquered in black.

Rick's popularity as a performer eventually led to a grueling schedule at a 400 seat music bar in Tampa called Rusty O'Reilly's, where he played with a five-piece band six nights a week from nine pm until three in the morning. He got paid in small amounts of cash and lots of beer and often, by the time he headed home in the wee hours, he was pretty trashed in more ways than one. After weeks of relentless playing and partying, Rick realized the heavy duty bar scene was not wearing well on his psyche or his body. He also remembered his Grandmother Delilah's admonitions, and with his growing awareness that many gifted musicians were burning out and dying of alcohol and drug abuse, he quit playing the bar scene and promised himself he'd never return to it. And he stuck to that promise. As Rick said with the seasoned smile of a 68 year old looking back over a long career, "It's hard to believe, but I've been playing music for 50 years now with the *same* liver!"

By the late 1970's, the pull of his native Green Mountain State was getting irresistibly strong. Rick began spending much of each summer performing back in Vermont and during the summer of 1978 he met a fellow named Leo Roy, a talented young musician from a farm family in South Royalton. They became friends and started playing together and soon formed The Bottom Dollar Band, which became very popular on the Vermont scene. Leo looked back on that exciting time with a smile, "After I met Rick, he lit me on fire and I couldn't wait to get into a band with him. He's a real 'Barnum and Bailey,' just an amazing promoter. He can go in and sell himself and his band and get money from a rock. We were so busy traveling all the time, playing and partying night and day that I don't know (or remember!) how we made it home from some gigs, especially when we'd do several back-to-back shows. People loved the band because we were a whole lot of fun to listen to. Rick and I played together for nearly 30 years till my arm gave out after a work injury, but we're still real good friends. There's nobody else around quite like him — anywhere."

One memorable show the band played was at the Crete Civic Center across the lake in Plattsburgh, New York. The band opened for country superstar Buck Owens, and Junior Sample, a popular, hayseed comedian from the hit TV show *Hee-Haw*. After their performance, the boys in the band squeezed into Rick's aging Pinto wagon and headed north to the town of Chazy for a gig the following day at the opening of a new gun club. True to form, Rick's car threw a rod and began spraying black motor oil all over the windshield. Leo laughed when he recalled that day. "We had to quick, turn on the windshield wipers to clear the oil enough so we could steer off the road. That damned car just shit the bed on us."

As he had done many times over his illustrious vehicular career, Rick wrestled the Pinto off the road into a ditch just as the engine burned up and seized. The band climbed up out of the ditch and stood on the side of the road trying to think of where they could stay for the night. Rick had a friend who owned a music store in Plattsburgh, so they hitched a ride to a phone booth and gave him a call. The man reluctantly said they all could sleep in his trailer for *one* night. Sweaty, tired and half full of beer, the Bottom Dollar Band piled into the poor fellow's trailer.

Leo continued, "We were stacked in that trailer tight as cord wood. What a crazy mess we were — farting, stinkin' and snoring all night! I can tell you that guy was awful glad to get rid of us as soon as the sun came up. Plus," Leo added with a mischievous smile, "there was no way in hell we were going to miss that gun club gig 'cause we'd heard they were going to have a real live Playboy bunny at it and we'd never seen one of those before."

The boys arrived at the gun club, cleaned up as best they could, and put on a great show. The place was jammed, the beer was flowing like a river and after awhile this voluptuous Playboy bunny arrives and gets up on stage to sing with the boys. Rick recalled trying to lead the band that day. "It was a real good time but it got pretty crazy. The guys were already going nuts *before* this smokin' hot girl got up on stage in her bunny suit, what little there was of it. Then she commenced to sing "Kansas City" at the top of her lungs. The place went through the roof and I can tell you it was a challenge for the Bottom Dollar boys to stay focused but somehow they managed to. Either that or the crowd was too drunk to know any different."

During those years, Rick also successfully marketed himself as "Rick Norcross and His Wonder Guitar." He was invited to host his own live radio program featuring his and other musicians' songs, working out of WKDR in Plattsburgh during the summers and WHBO in Tampa during the winters. "My show was modeled after traditional radio shows from the 1930's and 1940's, which were very popular and supported musicians by helping to attract bookings for live performances. It was a great way for musicians to showcase their material, build a loyal fan base and generate work. I had a really good circuit going in two markets for about ten years."

Rick had an extremely busy year in 1976, performing over 100 different shows. He also recorded an album at Dick Longfellow's Green Mountain Records, but, similar to the earlier album effort in Florida, his popular live performances didn't translate well onto vinyl and it was never released.

In the 1970's, Rick became increasingly interested in western swing music which he was first introduced to through Knocky Parker, who had played with the legendary Light Crust Doughboys. By the 1970's, a new, wildly popular band out of Austin, Texas, Asleep at the Wheel, was spreading western swing to the masses across America. Rick became enamored with the high energy, seven-piece arrangements of swing music, particularly with the songs of Asleep at the Wheel co-founder and fellow Vermonter, LeRoy Preston. As Rick spent more time playing in his own bands, he introduced several swing-type numbers and noticed that audiences loved the new music. In fact, during many shows audience members started getting up and dancing in front of the stage.

During his many years in Florida, Rick had connected with a Newport, Vermont native, Art Pepin, who owned the Budweiser beer distributorship in Tampa. Rick remembered Art as "a much loved, huge community-supporting guy, who was very helpful and enthusiastic with regard to me and my music. He booked my band into many company-related events and even helped fund my first successful album, *Nashfull.*"

Rick was able to return the favor to Art when he booked Rick's band to play at the *1984 Budweiser Pre-Super Bowl Party* just outside Tampa Stadium. That happened to be an extremely windy day, and one of the scheduled band's trucks was blown over on the interstate on the way to the show and that truck held the sound system for the event. They were unable to make it to Tampa Stadium, so Pepin's people called Rick and asked for help. Within a couple of hours, Rick had arranged for another professional sound system which was quickly delivered and set up. With the other band unable to play, Rick and his Nashfull Ramblers entertained the huge crowd most of the afternoon, to rave reviews. During the party, the celebratory football fans drank many truckloads of Budweiser beer kegs, 375 in all! The following weekend Rick's band played for 40,000 fans inside the stadium for Burt Reynolds's party celebrating the starting lineup for the Tampa Bay Bandits.

By the early 1980's, Rick had moved on from his dilapidated farm trucks and hearse days and became fascinated with the Nash Car Company, particularly with the automobiles they produced in the 1940's and '50's. He bought several Nashes including a 1952 Nash Rambler station wagon that served as his touring car and got him back and forth between Tampa and Vermont for many years. At that time George Romney (Mitt's father) owned the company and they were making a serious sports car, the highly collectable Nash Healey. The bodies of the Healeys were built in England then shipped to the US where American, Nash-built engines were installed.

Obsessed with these cars, Rick became the Publicity Chairman of the Nash Car Club of America. He even morphed his band into the Nashfull Ramblers, named for his Nash, which was always *full* of musical equipment (as well as snack wrappers, spent coffee cups and beer cans). "I bought several Nash cars over the years and they were usually beat to death by the time I got them. I really liked the design of them and got a charge out of driving them up and down the East Coast. Once in the early 1980's I was driving my 1950 Nash Ambassador from Florida to Vermont and encountered engine trouble near Aberdeen, Maryland. I always carried the roster of Nash Club members with me and I saw there was a collector named Leonard McGrady who lived nearby. I called him up and found out he had the largest collection of Nash Healeys in the world, as well as many used Nash parts. He had me come over that night and sleep on his couch. The next morning he gave me a wrench and let me remove the head off one of his junked Nashes and helped me install it on my disabled Ambassador. Thanks to him, I was off and running the rest of the way to Vermont."

Years later, Rick was given a special Rambler birthday gift by his friend and landlord, Harry Atkinson, who gave him the original neon sign from the local Rambler dealership which used to be on Riverside Avenue in Burlington. Harry had found the ten foot metal sign lying in a field in Monkton Village, Vermont and bought it for Rick. It has hung on the south end of Rick's home in the Railway Express building every since.

As busy as Rick was, it was still tough making a decent living just playing music. Not wanting to be tied down to another "real job" like he had at the *Tampa Times*, Rick worked hard at finding part-time event production jobs that would allow him enough time and money to keep performing his own music as often as possible. Deeply appreciative of the folks who had helped him get started in the music business, Rick also wanted to create as many good playing opportunities as possible for up and coming Vermont musicians. Little did he know that he was about to climb aboard a wild, 24 year long ride on his very own train called the *Green Mountain Chew Chew.*

Chapter Nine

A WILD RIDE ON THE *CHEW CHEW*

By the summer of 1983, Rick was back in Burlington looking to promote new events which would give his band and other regional acts new, higher profile venues at which to perform. He learned the Lake Champlain Regional Chamber of Commerce had put out a request for proposals to do a food-type festival during the month of June to try and stimulate business in the early part of Vermont's relatively short, but very important summer season. He researched the idea and discovered that Denver, Colorado had been successfully producing such an event so he communicated with the organizers, and learned as much as he could about how their festival worked. He then submitted a proposal for a family-friendly event that he called, *The Green Mountain Chew Chew Food and Music Festival*, and won the contract.

Rick's idea was to fill Burlington's City Hall Park with local food vendors, each selling bite-sized samples from their menu. In addition, there would be kids' activities and a stage featuring music and other kinds of entertainment. People would buy tickets to *ride* on the *Chew Chew* and move around the park turning in tokens at each food booth for a sample of their delicious offerings. During the first festival it unfortunately rained two of the three days and the Chamber lost money. Discouraged, they decided not to do another festival.

Rick, however, saw great potential in the event and was convinced he could turn it into a success. He bought the *Chew Chew* name and trademark and took on the responsibility of running the whole show.

Realizing the festival was going to be a major undertaking, Rick rented an office on the Burlington waterfront in the original Railway Express Depot building overlooking Perkins Pier on Lake Champlain. From his experiences working at the *Florida State Fair*, Rick knew he had to find major corporate sponsors to give the festival stable financial backing. He had previously made a connection with Ken Green, Director of Community Affairs at WCAX-TV, the local CBS affiliate and the largest television station in the state. Rick made an appointment to see Ken and brought him a photo that his grandmother Delilah had taken from the screen of her black and white TV set back in 1962. The photograph showed Rick and other Hardwick Academy students when they appeared on the station's show, *Dance Date*, a take-off of Dick Clark's *American Bandstand*, hosted by Ken. He loved the nostalgic photograph and after talking over Rick's ideas, became very enthusiastic about what this new event could do to promote the area and signed the station on as a sponsor.

In 1983, CBS's *Newhart* show, set in a fictitious Vermont town, was the most popular show on television, due in part to three hysterical woodchuck characters named Larry, his brother Darryl and his other brother, Darryl. Rick thought it would be great to bring the three actors to Burlington to perform a comedy routine at his first festival and was fortunate that Burlington radio station, WQCR (later WOKO) signed on to sponsor them. Once word spread that the *Newhart* stars were coming to the festival, Rick was certain people would come from all over the North Country to see them, and come they did.

Wanting to make his first *Chew Chew* as big an event as possible, Rick came up with an unusual idea for the actors' appearance. Based on a recent episode of the show, he talked the comedians into overseeing a competitive charity lard fight, in which local companies put together three-person teams that signed up ahead of time and donated an entrance fee. On the day of the event, a huge piece of slippery plastic was laid out on the north end of City Hall Park in the middle of which was a large washtub filled with a couple hundred pounds of lard donated by the John McKenzie Packing Company of Burlington.

With WQCR broadcasting live from the scene, brightly dressed teams of three grabbed handfuls of lard, and with bull's eyes taped to their shirts, lined up back-to-back. On a signal, they took ten paces away from each other, turned and fired their lard balls at the opposing team. The messy competition was great fun and finally, when only one local team was left standing, they competed against the ultimate team – Larry, Darryl, and Darryl.

The competition raised over $1500 which was donated to one of WQCR's major charities, *The Children's' Miracle Network*. Rick remembered the great lard fight with a laugh. "It was really something to see. There were probably a thousand people watching this crazy thing which pretty much turned downtown into a lard bath. When it was over and the local team was able to knock Larry, Darryl and Darryl out of the competition, the place went nuts. Kids dove into that washtub and scooped out every last bit of lard. They flung it everywhere – over the vendors' tents and into the crowd, into the street, onto unsuspecting cars and tourists – it was mayhem. But you know, what was really cool was that people had such fun with crazy things back then and not a single person complained about getting into the mess. They just laughed and screamed (and ran!) and appreciated it for what it was, which was having fun to raise money for a good cause. Folks were mercifully way less up-tight back then and we were all the better for it.

"Though many people seemed to enjoy the *Chew Chew* idea, the first year I ran it was pretty rough going. I changed the system from tickets to wooden tokens with the idea that we would keep the finances simple by having the food vendors turn in their tokens which would be weighed and the vendors paid accordingly. Once again the weather did not cooperate and it rained – a lot. Then some of the food vendors soaked their tokens in water making their pay-out weight substantially more than they were entitled to, so we ended up losing money again. On the other hand, most of the vendors were super to work with and I met some *very* enjoyable people that became the core of my crew. I saw what great potential this sort of event had and wanted to develop it further."

With the help of many talented Vermont restaurateurs and local musicians, the festival grew into a terrific annual event. Within a few years, though, it became so time consuming Rick could no longer return to Tampa in the winter. He sold El Rancho Tedioso in Tampa and moved permanently into the old Railway Express Depot and affectionately named it Rambler Ranch. As interest in the *Chew Chew* grew, Rick was able to get many local businesses involved, including toward the end of its run, Sam Mazza's Farms. Mazza's sponsored their own stage featuring everything from Peggy Thompson's mouth-watering strawberry demonstrations to the Coconut Grove Steel Drum Band and Mango Jam, both of which delighted crowds with their upbeat mix of Caribbean calypso, Zydeco and Louisiana Cajun music. Mazza's stage also featured a *Kid's Olympics*, filled with fun-loving children's games hosted by Charlie Papillo, a popular radio personality from local station, WVMT. After a few successful years, businesses and patrons alike looked forward to starting the summer season off with a fun-filled ride on the *Chew Chew*.

As the festival gained in size and popularity, it outgrew City Hall Park and became the first event to be featured at Burlington's newly developed Waterfront Park. Over its 24 years, the *Chew Chew* drew hundreds of thousands of people to Burlington from all over the northeast and was a favorite early summer destination for visitors from Montreal, Boston, New York, and beyond. As Rick said about his "favorite family-oriented feeding frenzy," "Everybody likes to eat and the combination of great food and the cream of Vermont music delivered in a world-class setting made the festival a very special experience for locals and tourists alike. Despite our many challenges, not least of which was our fickle Vermont weather, people seemed to have a blast."

One of the great things about the food festival was its focus on introducing new types of cuisines to the Burlington area. Each vendor had to offer three unique items on their menu and there could be no overlap with other vendors. Additionally, everyone served at least one new menu item each year to keep the offerings fresh and interesting. One of the most popular offerings was a spicy Cajun menu introduced by Art and Manon O'Connor's small local eatery, The Bourbon Street Grill. According to Rick, the Grill's success at the *Chew Chew* catapulted it into being one of Burlington's and the festival's favorite restaurants for many years. By the end of its run, the festival had showcased the offerings of over 400 area restaurants and food producers, who sold an astounding 3.7 million dollars worth of food in exchange for those fifty-cent tokens. That's over 7 million tokens.

Rick's friend, Harry Atkinson, spoke of the importance of the *Chew Chew*. "Rick took the idea of promoting local restaurants to the general public and made it affordable for people from all walks of life to get a taste of many different types of food. That was 25 years before the concept of *localvore* hit the streets and before all the push to support local businesses. And he did it on a shoestring budget and a wallet full of air."

The festival also showcased a diverse collection of music. Rick brought in most of the major musicians from Vermont as well as other national performers he knew from his years of being on tour, including Commander Cody, Gidget & Gandhi, Tommy Overstreet, the Gibson Brothers, Banjo Dan and the Midnite Plowboys, John Cassel, Jon Gailmor, the Starline Rhythm Boys, Tammy Fletcher and The Disciples, Big Joe Burrell & The Unknown Blues Band, and The Throbulators. Rick also showcased folk legend, Jonathan Edwards of "Sunshine" fame, and during one *Chew Chew*, held an *International Folk Festival*, which featured artists that Rick had met touring in England, including Carolyn Hester and English folk club owner, Derek Sarjeant and his wife, Hazel. For those artists traveling from afar, Rick arranged for sponsors to cover their airfare and other expenses.

Over the years, the *Chew Chew* attracted national attention from as far away as California, where the *Los Angeles Times* featured it in their Travel Section. The

Philadelphia Inquirer named it a "Top Ten Festival," and it was featured both in *Boston Magazine* and by AAA, as a great "New England Getaway."

In order to run such a complicated event, which catered to nearly 20,000 people over three days, Rick had to have a talented, dedicated, and above all, fun-loving crew. There were many people that had a hand in bringing the *Chew Chew* to life, but two in particular stand out, in more ways than one. The first is Creighton Smith, a Burlington restaurateur who, at the time he became involved in the festival, was owner of the Vermont Pasta Company, which operated both a fresh pasta factory and a busy catering business. When he heard about the *Chew Chew*, he thought it was a great promotional platform for local businesses and his company became a regular vendor at the festival. Creighton had a terrific time at the festival and soon got his whole family involved working as part of the event's crew.

Creighton remembered those days fondly. "Rick has a way of getting people real excited about things and after getting to know him a little, we all just jumped on board the *Chew Chew*. The core group of us were a bunch of 'classy carnies' that worked really hard getting the festival up and running each day and played just as hard when it would shut down for the night. The bottom line is we had *so much fun* working for Rick, who ran around in his cowboy hat all weekend directing and entertaining everyone – staff and customers alike."

As smoothly as the *Chew Chew Festival* appeared to run on the outside, Creighton remembered feeling they were always flirting with disaster behind the scenes. One year in particular Waterfront Park was deluged with rain the day before the festival was to open. The entire area became so waterlogged that the lawns where the tents stood were completely under water. Knowing they had to be up and running the next day, all the crew members set about with rollers and brooms *squeegee-ing* the rain water out of the festival area and into the city's storm drains. They worked all night, laying down dry hay and building plywood walkways so people could move around without getting wet. Creighton recalled, "By daybreak we were totally exhausted, both from the hard work and the endless jokes, sarcasm and laughter that was the glue that kept us all together no matter what the weather threw at us. Looking back, I am amazed at what we were able to pull off. And I wouldn't have missed a minute of it."

For Creighton and his family, the *Chew Chew* became an annual, cherished event. His kids were only six when they first became involved. "For one festival we put together a new booth called, 'Berry Good Stuff,' from which we sold all kinds of delicious strawberry treats. Our kids' hands would be bright red for days from shucking over 150 flats of fresh, juicy strawberries from Sam Mazza Farms. I remember we dressed one of our kids in a homemade strawberry costume with our booth number on it and he scurried around the festival grounds drumming up business, getting people to follow him to our booth. Even when they got older, our kids continued to work for Rick as regular crew members at the festival for years."

Friends for many years, Creighton had great respect for Rick's ability to bring a wide diversity of people together to have fun and appreciate the finer things in life. "Over his career, Rick Norcross has touched every level of society from senators and world famous musicians to the dishwashers working in our restaurant, and he treats them all with the same respect. He believes that nobody is better than anyone else. He is also a tremendous history buff who knows a ton about Vermont and Lake Champlain, especially its great steamboats, and loves to share his enthusiasm with others, especially through his original songs. The other thing I really admire is Rick's unwavering focus on music. No matter what is going on, no matter the hardships he has had to walk through, music is always at the heart of his life. It's awesome to have such a lifelong passion and freely share it with everyone else."

Creighton credits another talented and highly-spirited local, Barbara Bardin, as the person who largely kept the crew of the *Chew Chew*, and its conductor Rick, on track. Affectionately known as "P-Bear," Barb joined the crew early on and everyone quickly realized not only how much fun she was to be around but also how valuable she was as a worker. She soon became the chief mechanic of the festival and Rick gave her a custom wooden toolbox filled with a variety of *tools* she used to fix the innumerable problems that would develop behind the scenes. Creighton chuckled. "Back then Rick wasn't quite as polished, shall we say, as he later became, and his sometimes sharp tongue could get him headed into a heap trouble. It seemed that P-Bear was always the one who was right there to steer him out of a jam, somehow fix things and get people laughing again. She is an amazing woman and one of my best friends."

Rick and Barb, who both had a tremendous sense of humor, met in the 1970's when she was selling lingerie at Burlington's premiere Church Street woman's shop, Bertha Church. A self-described "Corsetiere and Boobalogist," she specialized in fitting women for bras and girdles and for *some reason* Rick loved to visit her at work. She remembered back to those days. "Rick would weasel his way into the shop and just hang around and make me laugh for hours. And nobody seemed to mind because he's an exceptionally interesting and quick-witted guy who was *so* much fun to be around. Also, under the laughter, we both had experienced tough, painful childhoods and being able to share some of that with each other helped us develop a deep bond."

When Rick started the *Chew Chew*, Barb loved the whole idea and soon became an indispensible member of the crew. She recalled, "Working the *Chew Chew* was like going to 'Carnie Camp' every summer. It was totally chaotic and a ton of hard work but it was a blast — like we were working at Coney Island or something." Barb was very bright and able to sense what needed to be done to keep the *Chew Chew* running smoothly, so everyone, including Rick, came to depend upon her. Her antics became part of the festival's tradition including her penchant for luring good-humored local police officers into the fun. "The camaraderie at the heart of the festival was wonderful," Barb recalled, "like nothing Burlington had ever seen before. For three days, thousands of people from all over the place felt like they were part of something really fun and creative and it all came out of Rick's extremely imaginative mind. He really did amazing things for this area."

The *Chew Chew* carnies' after-hours shenanigans became legendary as they cast themselves upon local bars, raucously partying late into the night. One of their favorite haunts was the infamous, and now defunct, Chicken Bone Café, which Barb affectionately referred to as, *"Chez Bone-aire."* Well-lubricated with summer libations, the crew laughed the night away, dancing on the stage, on tables and out into the street, getting just enough sleep to open the festival on time the next morning.

Once the Burlington *Chew Chew* had become a resounding success, Rick and his crew decided to try the same kind of festival in Bennington, Vermont, and Plattsburgh, New York. Barb laughed as she recalled those days. "When we took it on the road things got even crazier. We all stayed together in some god-forsaken, unsuspecting local motel where we partied our brains out. We usually took over the motel's pool, drinking and skinny-dipping till the wee hours of the morning. Over in Plattsburgh, it was more of the same — working hard all day and partying most of the night. Some of the rather provincial locals that Rick hired on didn't seem to know what had hit them!"

After their all-night partying, one of the crew's favorite places to land in Plattsburgh was a local drive-up establishment called the Toot and Tell 'Em, where you blew your horn, they'd come out and you'd tell them what you wanted to eat and drink. The crew would jam into a couple of rigs, pull up and *toot* for a couple rounds of strong hot coffee which was badly needed to once again get the *Chew Chew* up and running.

Barb had deep admiration and respect for Rick. "He is truly a fascinating character, a legend really. For someone of his musical stature, who has traveled and performed all over the place, he is a unique and very sensitive person. And he loves to share his wealth of information about music and history and his keen observations of people. Rick's soul runs deep and he is extraordinarily creative. He's not someone you can do a fly-by on. The magnitude of his being makes you want to keep learning more about him. That's one reason so many people have been attracted to him from all over the world. Plus, he's one hellova lot of fun!"

Rick and his crew became good friends and continued their adventures even after the festival season. After he sold his pasta company, Creighton took a job as a salesman for a large food distributor and one summer decided to entertain a visiting wholesale supplier by taking him to Montreal to Chez Paree, a high class *gentleman's club* known for its provocative entertainment. Creighton thought it would spice things up if they took Rick and some of his other *Chew Chew* friends along and, of course, they were delighted to oblige.

Rick dressed for the occasion in his very best, classic black western outfit, complete with polished cowboy boots, wide-brimmed hat and dark shades. Creighton rented a stretch limousine, picked Rick up at the Ranch and they all headed north. They'd had several cocktails by the time they crossed the Canadian border on their way to the bright lights of Montreal. As they entered the city, Creighton had the great idea that Rick — dressed as he was — should pretend he was Hank Williams, Jr. stopping at the Chez Paree on his way to perform a concert at the Montreal Forum.

Creighton recalled, "We got totally into it, and the limo driver pulls right up on the sidewalk in front of this fancy club and another guy and I get out with shades on and act like we are Mr. William's security detail. Rick and the others stayed in the limo while we checked out the area, speaking into our non-existent lapel microphones. After we determined the area was safe, we approached the doorman, who was dressed in a very fancy uniform and told him we needed VIP seating for Hank Williams and seven other people in his party. The doorman, who seemed used to catering to celebrities, spoke into *his* microphone and in a minute or so, motioned for us to follow him. We opened the limo door and Rick, with his fancy cowboy hat and sunglasses on, stepped onto the sidewalk like the world's biggest superstar.

"So this big security guy takes us past the bouncers, down to the very front of the club and seats us on a set of plush leather couches right next to the stage. Rick played the part to the nines, nodding to people who by then have heard the buzz that he's Hank Williams, Jr. The management of Chez Paree immediately brought us complimentary drinks and treated us like royalty. Rick flawlessly held court as the resident celebrity for a couple of hours before he had to leave to perform at the Forum. We had an amazing time and, despite many drinks, were somehow able to keep it together and not blow our cover. When we finally left, we piled back into the limo, completely cracked up and had the driver take us, not to the Forum, but to a seedy club that was a little more our speed, called Wicked Wanda's. I gotta' say, those times were some of the most fun I've ever had."

During the early *Chew Chew* years, serendipitously working in Rick's building was a woman named Marilyn, who was the sister of highly respected western swing singer and songwriter, LeRoy Preston. LeRoy had left his band, Asleep at the Wheel, in 1979, after many grueling years on the road and had returned to his native Vermont. But after a year and a half he was lured back to the music business and moved to Nashville to work at Bug Music, his top-flight publishing company. He continued to write songs, including hits for Roseanne Cash, K.D. Lang and others including, "My Baby Thinks She's a Train," "I Wonder," and "Full Moon Full of Love."

Knowing they would enjoy each other, Marilyn introduced Rick to her brother, LeRoy, and they immediately hit it off. After they met, Rick helped LeRoy reassemble the first band he ever played in while growing up near Barre, Vermont, in the 1960's. The band was called The VIP's, and Rick gave them a spot playing at his *Chew Chew* Festival. He also recorded their performance and made it into a CD. LeRoy remembered, "That CD is one of my favorite recordings of anything I've ever done and it happened because Rick cared enough to put it together. I am very grateful that Rick gave me and so many others opportunities to play up here in Vermont. Between the hundreds of performances with his band and the many festivals he's produced over the years, Rick created a long-standing platform for musicians to play on that otherwise wouldn't have existed. The truth was, I co-founded and played with the most famous western swing band on the planet, but I considered Rick Norcross to be one of my biggest supporters. He's just a very generous guy, always working to encourage and promote other musicians right along with his own career."

Rick continued to spend more time playing with his band, which he renamed Rick and the Ramblers Western Swing Band. The Ramblers established itself as the premier band of its type in the Northeast, performing a combination of different types of music, including traditional Bob Wills material as well as songs popularized and written by LeRoy and Rick. The seven-piece Ramblers brought together some of the finest musicians in the area and created a top shelf, professional show. There had never been a true western swing band in Vermont and audiences loved the up-tempo, danceable amalgamation of country, folk, blues and jazz. By the late 1980's, the Ramblers seemed to be playing everywhere, from the *Champlain Valley Fair* and the *WOKO Country Music Festival*, to the *Vermont Dairy Festival* in Enosburg Falls. They also headlined the *Tunbridge World's Fair*, as well as the *Addison County, Essex and Milton Fairs.* They played the *Chew Chew Festival* multiple times, were featured at a Canadian hot air balloon festival, and performed at *Vermont Day* at the Big E exposition in Springfield, MA, New England's largest fair. In the winter, Rick even took the band south to play week-long engagements at the *Florida State Fair.*

Rick and his Ramblers were on a roll. Soon, he decided his band deserved to travel in style, and he wouldn't rest until he found them a very special set of wheels.

Chapter Ten

THE RAMBLERS HAVE ARRIVED

In 1985, when Rick and LeRoy Preston got together, they were at quite different stages in their careers. LeRoy was tired of the high-pressure road life with his band, Asleep at the Wheel, and was also wearing down working as a songwriter in Nashville. "I'd been around and played the big time a lot but I'm not sure I'd ever met anyone like Rick Norcross. He was so welcoming, so enthusiastic and engaging. I'm a songwriter, pride myself on it and do it well. But I'm like tunnel vision compared to Rick, who always has a sense of the bigger picture. He can do it all: he plays, performs, produces, and writes great material, especially his old Vermont-type songs. He could write with anybody in Nashville – he's that good. And he has encyclopedic knowledge of Vermont history which he blends into everything he does.

"When I finally moved back to Vermont I'd done a million miles on those Asleep at the Wheel tour buses and couldn't wait to get off. And then I met this incredibly energetic guy who couldn't wait to buy his band a bus and get on it! The Ramblers were really getting popular and Rick was determined to put his band on a classic tour bus."

Rick fondly remembered traveling with the Florida Southern College chorus choir in Flxible tour buses, so when it came time to buy the Ramblers their own bus, he started looking for that same type of classic vehicle. To his surprise, he found a 1946 Flxible Airporter bus in the back of a dumpster lot near the Burlington International Airport. His friend Dan Dubonnet helped him buy the bus and Rick proudly drove it home to the waterfront. Unfortunately, the fellow he bought it from didn't tell him there was a metal air deflector missing, which was essential to adequately cool the large engine. Before Rick could make it the few miles home to Rambler Ranch, the engine overheated and blew in the middle of Main Street in Burlington, thus continuing his tortured love affair with old vehicles. Never to be deterred, Rick soon found a replacement engine, talked a local mechanic into switching it out for the blown engine, and the band appeared to have a new home on the road.

Traveling on the '46 Flxible wasn't exactly smooth sailing, as LeRoy recalled with a chuckle. "With that first dilapidated rig of his, Rick had the name of the band painted only on the ditch side of the bus because they would usually get part way to a gig and something would clank or grind or a vital part would break loose and fall onto the road. The damn thing would conk out and end up in the ditch – again. Then the whole band would have to climb off the bus and hitchhike to the gig, but remarkably they usually showed up on time and rarely missed a beat. I'm guessing after a while most passersby knew it was the Ramblers' bus even if they couldn't see the name on it."

After a short, eventful life, the *new* engine also blew on the way to a music festival in Crown Point, New York. Mercifully, this time Rick couldn't find the parts to fix it so he had to "put it down." Still determined to find his band a proper tour bus, he then located a rare 1957 Flxible Starliner that a man in Massachusetts needed to sell for financial reasons. The Starliner was quite a fancy model and that particular bus had been converted at great expense from an intercity bus to a custom private coach for a wealthy individual and, as Rick says, "it ran like a watch." He was able to cobble together $12,000 and bought the green beauty which the band affectionately named the *Pickle.* It has been the band's faithful bus ever since.

With the Ramblers in full swing, so to speak, Rick was extremely busy booking gigs and playing in the band, as well as running the *Chew Chew*, which became an almost fulltime job itself. Despite his full schedule, and sensing an opportunity, in 1991 he approached the State of Vermont about writing and recording an album for its upcoming bicentennial celebration. The State liked the idea, so he brought together a talented group of Vermont musicians including Paul Asbell, "Banjo" Dan Lindner, LeRoy Preston, Peter Riley, and Alan Davis. They wrote what became the official song of the Vermont Bicentennial, "You Can't Get There From Here." Recorded at Chas Eller Studios in Burlington, the CD came out for the bicentennial and the Ramblers performed it at the celebration and street dance on the Statehouse lawn in Montpelier that August. Two years later, Rick and the Ramblers played at Howard Dean's Inaugural Governor's Ball, long before he became a presidential candidate.

Once he had moved to Burlington fulltime, Rick became involved in many activities around the Lake Champlain area, including a group of local steamboat aficionados, originally led by retired Lake Champlain Transportation Captain, Merritt Carpenter. The group, which continued to meet most every week for 30 years, completely restored a beautiful Fantail Sloop which originally had an 1893 Shipman one-cylinder steam engine, powered by a Porcupine Boiler. The group worked on the engine with the help of Rick's close friend, Harry Atkinson, an international boiler specialist who also owned the building Rick lived in and where the sloop was housed. The men eventually became nervous about the safety of the steam engine, and replaced it with a converted electric motor from a Basin Harbor Club golf cart. The sleek *Merritt E. Carpenter* could be seen gracefully plying the waters of Burlington Harbor just as the *Ticonderoga* had nearly a century before. And while Captain Carpenter died years ago, Rick remained friends with his widow, "Kit," whom, in her late nineties, he took grocery shopping every Sunday morning year round.

Living on the Burlington waterfront, Rick fell back in love with the Champlain Valley and with his beloved *Ticonderoga* in particular. He began collecting all types of memorabilia from the great steamboat including original tickets, a lifebuoy, broadsides advertising her many excursions on the lake, and a full set of custom blue and white china used to serve elegant meals onboard in the 1920's and 1930's. Long interested in Vermont history and antiques, Rick gradually started turning his lakeside home into a veritable museum filled with antiques and artifacts from Vermont. Looking back, he credited growing up at the Shelburne Museum with "infecting him with the collecting bug and a reverence for history" that influenced many of the most important accomplishments of his life.

One of Rick's collecting interests was related to learning that his childhood neighbor, Mary Lee, at Fort Ethan Allen, was actually a singer and movie star from the 1930's and 1940's. He started studying her life and discovered that once she left Hollywood in 1945, she kept her early celebrity a secret as she was burned out with the spotlight and wanted to live a normal life with her new army sergeant husband. Her career had started as a young girl during the Great Depression when her cash-strapped parents pushed her into a grueling singing career. She was cute and personable and had a great voice, so audiences took to her and she spent many years on the road touring with such popular acts as the Ted Weems Orchestra and other big bands. In her teens, she was discovered by Warner Brothers Pictures who hired her to appear in their *Nancy Drew* movies. She then moved to Republic Pictures where she was billed as "America's Little Sister," and her popularity grew exponentially. She starred with famous cowboy singer, Gene Autry, in nine movies and then, when he left to serve in World War II, went on to appear alongside Roy Rogers in three more films.

Rick looked back. "Mary Lee was a very talented woman who, unfortunately, had been worked to death acting and singing back when she was just a girl. And it was too bad as they'd just used her up by the time she was twenty, but luckily she'd had the fortitude to quit, get out and move to Vermont. I was pretty young at the time, but I remember her as my mother's friend and she seemed to always be at our kitchen table. Ironically, though, it was many years after we lived next to her that I actually came to appreciate who she was."

Rick started collecting movie posters and memorabilia from Mary Lee and Gene Autry movies, and displayed them on the walls at Rambler Ranch along with many items from the *Ticonderoga*, including a large wooden replica of the steamboat which is mounted above his bed.

During the early 1990's, in between gigs and festivals, Rick continued to collect classic music items like a set of gold records made in the shape of guitars for hits recorded by country star Johnny Horton in the 1950's. Even the rug on Rick's living room floor came from the home of Audrey Williams, widow of Hank Williams, Sr., and was used during the time Hank, Jr. was a young boy.

On Rick's living room wall hung the 19th Century clock Harold Patch gave to Rick for painting his house during his honeymoon. On a table in Rick's studio sat an old reel-to-reel tape deck that held a recording of Mr. Patch describing in riveting detail a chance encounter with Champ, the legendary Lake Champlain monster. Many years before, he and his wife had stopped at a lakeside rest area in Alburgh, Vermont, and were having a picnic lunch when the great serpent appeared offshore. On the recording, Mr. Patch's steady, provincial voice was enough to convince anyone that Champ was alive and well. Rick reflected on his museum-like home. "I not only like all this old stuff and think it's so important to preserve for future generations, I also just really love the feel of it around me, the classic ambience it affords."

After Mr. Patch died, Rick kept in touch with his daughter, Lorraine, who had preserved her father's collection of books by renowned Vermont writer, Rowland E. Robinson. Lorraine kindly gave the books to Rick, who remembered Mr. Patch reading them to his blind children in East Hardwick. Rick read every one of the books with interest and became fascinated with Robinson, who was considered an accomplished folklorist. He had written a number of books about a fictitious Vermont town named, Danvis, and was also known nationally as a professional illustrator whose drawings appeared regularly in magazines such as *Forest and Stream* and *Atlantic Monthly*. Late in his life, Rowland Robinson became blind himself, and was only able to continue writing by dictating his stories to his wife who transcribed them for him. Studying Robinson and his interesting family deepened Rick's love for Vermont folklore and history and gave him fodder for new songs.

While Rick struggled with early attempts at recording his comedic folk songs, once he formed a band and moved into western swing music, he and the Ramblers hit their stride. In 1993, Rick and LeRoy Preston put together a collection of songs for a new CD entitled, *Can't Catch a Rambler.* It featured individually written songs by Rick and LeRoy, as well as some they wrote together. LeRoy was still working at Bug Music, so Rick went down to Nashville, where he did the pre-production work on the album with LeRoy. The album featured upbeat swing tunes, and when it was released the next year, it was well received. After nearly 30 years of writing and performing songs, Rick finally produced a recording he was proud of and one that found an enthusiastic audience.

By 1998, the Ramblers were on tour throughout the summer months, including playing gigs at Vermont state parks on weekends. Visitors to the parks enjoyed the Ramblers so much that the State continued hiring the band to play five shows each summer through 2011, performing 59 concerts in all. Some locals became so attached to the band that they traveled from park to park following the Ramblers around the state throughout the summer. Always welcoming audience participation, the band often helped their regulars celebrate birthdays, anniversaries or other events during their shows. Longtime fan, Elaine Russell of Vergennes said, "Rick and the Ramblers make you feel like you're a part of their family. They are *so* much fun to listen to. Even my little granddaughter loves to get up and dance to their music." Remarkably, Elaine and her family made it to every one of the band's State Park shows for four years straight.

When he could, Rick also spent time back at the Shelburne Museum, which was approaching its half-century anniversary. With his deep childhood ties to the museum and his expertise with event production, Rick was hired to produce and play at the museum's *First Fifty Birthday Party* in 1997. The hugely successful event set the all-time attendance record at the museum with over 14,000 people attending the festivities.

The following year Rick produced and the Ramblers played at the museum's *Ticonderoga Restoration Party*, another major event which marked the end of an extensive renovation of the magnificent steamboat. For that celebration, Rick brought in the great composer and steamboat captain, John Hartford and his band, as well as St. Albans, Vermont's, Sterling Weed's Imperial Orchestra, and the Vermont Jazz Ensemble. The day long celebration was capped off with spectacular fireworks over the *Ti* that night.

In 2001 the Ramblers recorded another CD entitled, *I Heard the Highway*. The title song, penned by LeRoy Preston, was about how he came to leave his Vermont farm for the city in the 1960's. Songs from the CD got good airplay on northern New England and New York radio stations, including WDEV, "The Voice of Vermont" in Waterbury. Longtime WDEV radio personality, Jack Donovan, frequently played the album on his show which helped the Ramblers' get their new recording out to a large audience. Donovan had been a steadfast supporter of Rick for many years and was one of the first to feature him, singing on his station's original live radio show back in 1976.

"Rick's a very thoughtful guy," Jack said, "a loyal friend and one of the most talented and funny people I've ever met. Through his music and festivals he's brought so many people together over the years and helped a lot of musicians get their careers going. He has given them great showcases – like the *Chew Chew Festival* – in which to play and get great exposure. He's always surrounded himself with terrific musicians and writes some great original songs about a Vermont that seems to be long gone." Jack chuckled. "My wife and I have had so much fun with Rick over the years. Back in the 1970's we used to call him "The Tampa Chicken," because he'd play up here during the summers but head back to Florida at the first snowflake. Eventually, he had to come back to Vermont fulltime which didn't surprise me. This has always been his real home."

In addition to performing, over the years Rick taught himself how to make creative, computer-generated graphics, producing colorful and effective advertising for several local businesses including Sam Mazza Farms, Cloud Nine Fishing Charters, and the Vermont Railway System. This sideline allowed him to make enough of a living to keep music at the forefront of his life. Rick's involvement in the Burlington community also continued to deepen as he volunteered for several civic organizations including the Burlington Business Association, the Vermont Leadership Institute, First Night Burlington and the South End Arts and Business Association, sponsors of the area's popular annual *Art Hop.*

Burlington City Council President, Joan Shannon, complimented Rick as a wonderful, people-oriented person with a unique combination of creative skills. "Rick knows the connection between the arts and business and how to effectively lobby the powers that be to get good things done. He has set his roots deep in our community and his tireless dedication has resulted in many friendships, and great respect and admiration from a multitude of folks. Rick doesn't look at his work as a job, but as a lifelong part of who he is."

Among many others who have sung Rick's praises is Kathy Soula, a marketing and media specialist from Free Press Media, owner of the *Burlington Free Press* that Rick once delivered before school in Shelburne. She said, "I never stop marveling at Rick's creativity and ability to build a brand. And what I admire most about him is his curiosity and commitment to lifelong learning and his ability to maintain good relationships for a lifetime."

In 2005, in recognition of his many years of devoted service to the community, Burlington Mayor Peter Clavelle declared March 23, Rick's 60th birthday, "Rick Norcross Day." On the official proclamation, he wrote: "Rick Norcross from a young age has promoted music, harmony, happiness and public good throughout his life [and] has served this community with distinction and generosity and never missed an opportunity to contribute his time and talents to hundreds of community events and organizations. Rick Norcross is a

Hardwick boy who never turns his back on his roots. I encourage all citizens to honor him for his tireless contributions. "

After returning to Vermont fulltime, Rick began "living his dream." He developed a great balance in his life, at the forefront of which was playing with his beloved Ramblers. Little did he know who was about to walk onto that hallowed Rambler stage.

Chapter Eleven

TARYN AND THE BLUE GARDENIAS

In addition to playing his own music, Rick loved listening to performances of a wide range of other musicians. One night in 2006 he went to hear a female jazz quartet featuring Vermont songstress, Taryn Noelle, backed up by Rambler guitar player, Dono Schabner. Rick was captivated by Taryn's beautiful voice and her entrancing stage presence and immediately felt she might be a great addition to the Ramblers. Two weeks later, he called Taryn and asked her to come by the Ranch to try out a few songs together. Their voices and personalities blended beautifully and they thoroughly enjoyed each other. Feeling she would compliment the music of his band, Rick asked Taryn to join the Ramblers for a show and the audience loved her.

Taryn fit into the band so well Rick asked her to join them as their female vocalist for their 2007 summer tour. Taryn remembered getting to know the Ramblers' iconic front man. "Before I met Rick, I certainly knew of him but had no idea what an amazing man he is. Rick is an original with a huge, instantly warm heart. He makes everyone feel included and treats everyone – band and audience – like family because that's how he thinks of them. There's no one else like him. He has such character and *is* such a character." Taryn paused and laughed. "Can you imagine how much fun it was for me the first time I rode on the *Pickle* to perform at a show? Here I am, this jazz singer and actress who's suddenly dressed up in a cool cowgirl outfit with western boots and big red sunglasses, riding on that classic Starliner tour bus to a state park date with a great bunch of guys who are incredibly funny. I am so fond of them and appreciate that they have always been very inclusive of me as usually the only woman on board. I am *so* fortunate to be a part of Rick's ongoing, legendary story. And I also greatly appreciate all the fantastic musicians and musical styles Rick has supported over the years. He has been a creative bridge between so many people, musicians and audiences alike. I don't think northern New England would even know what western swing music was if it wasn't for Rick Norcross."

By the spring of 2008, Rick was ready to record his next album, the sixth on his own Airflyte Records label. The CD was titled, *I Rode the Ti - Songs from the Heart of Vermont.* The title song, written by Rick, pays homage to the steamboat and recalls riding on that last voyage on Lake Champlain in November of 1954, when he was living at the Shelburne Museum. By the time Rick and the band were ready to record, Taryn had become part of a new jazz trio, The Blue Gardenias, with two other accomplished Vermont singers, Juliet McVicker and Amber deLaurentis. Rick asked the Gardenias to be his special guests on the new album which resulted in a wonderful blending of classic western swing numbers, a Gene Autry movie number, and six original songs written by Rick.

That summer the Blue Gardenias joined the Ramblers at a benefit concert to help raise money to replace the aging granite steps of the Hardwick Town House. It was a hot Sunday afternoon and the first time they had all sung together in a live performance. Taryn recalled what a great experience it was. "The Gardenias and the Ramblers just harmonized so beautifully. And after all the miles he's traveled, hearing Rick do his original and often very funny folk songs from over 40 years there in his hometown was very moving. It was amazing to be a part of that, singing with this big-hearted legend."

The *Norcross Homecoming Concert* was reported in the Hardwick Gazette like this: "Despite a bad cold, Norcross couldn't contain his enthusiasm and excitement at being in his home town. And the trio that was with him was a joy to hear with their beautiful sound." Performing that fundraising concert meant a great deal to Rick, who had always maintained close ties with Hardwick. Throughout his years working in Tampa, he came up during the summers to visit as much as possible. He also kept in touch by writing letters to Harold Patch, his grandmother Delilah and to his Aunt Suzie Eastman, who owned the East Hardwick General Store. In one letter he told her that he couldn't wait to spend more time back in "Vermont, home sweet home."

The Ramblers' *I Rode the Ti* CD was a success and one of Rick's original songs, "A Grill, A Bumper, Four Headlights, and a $50 Bill," got national airplay on NPR's popular *Car Talk* show out of Boston featuring Click and Clack, The Tappet Brothers.

By 2009, Rick was involved with music almost fulltime, which left little time and energy for other endeavors. Also, despite its ongoing popularity, the costs of producing the *Chew Chew Festival* had skyrocketed and over the years the event had fallen on hard financial times. The price of tent and stage rentals along with high utility and permit costs made it extremely difficult to make any profit. Then in 2009, the festival was once again hit with devastating rain, resulting in a loss of over $20,000.

Rick knew he couldn't keep the festival going, but wanted to thank all the sponsors, vendors, visitors, and crew that had made it such a wonderful success, so he decided to put on one final festival which he called the "Last Supper." Thousands of people came to enjoy that final festival and to the disappointment of many, the *Chew Chew* ended its long run on June 28th of 2009. To Rick's surprise, Burlington Mayor Bob Kiss issued a Mayoral Proclamation declaring July 2009 as "Rick Norcross and The Green Mountain Chew Chew Month," in appreciation for "the long and successful run of this important cultural event." Rick was further heartened as he receive congratulatory phone calls and letters from the entire Vermont congressional delegation.

Many of the musicians who played the *Chew Chew* expressed gratitude for what Rick had accomplished. One of those is Rockabilly recording artist, Rosie Flores, who first met Rick through LeRoy Preston as he and Rosie were both signed to Bug Music as their publisher. "I played the *Chew Chew* festival a couple of times and really appreciated Rick's love for western swing and country music. He always treated me with the utmost respect and basically went out of his way to make sure when I came to play in Burlington that everything was high class and top notch. He is a Top of the Mark guy as a band leader, a musician, and friend."

One would think that over the years of producing the *Chew Chew*, Rick would have secured his financial future. In reality, he had spent most of his money hiring a kaleidoscope of musicians to perform. As LeRoy Preston said, "Rick was not only totally dedicated to showcasing excellent local musicians, he would bear any expense to bring in the very best national acts, sometimes to his own financial detriment."

Dan Dubonnet, general manager of Burlington's Hall Communications, which owns WOKO, agreed. "All those years Rick was so dedicated to supporting musicians and creating great opportunities for people to play and to enjoy music, he didn't pay himself nearly enough. He was just so happy to be doing the music thing that he didn't really take care of himself. Ironically, though, it's a huge part of his charm and something to be admired. His life has never been about fame and fortune; it's always been about the music and getting it out to as many people as possible. It is remarkable the tremendous positive influence he has had over his career both through playing his own music and through his many different festivals. That's why we at WOKO are proud to have been a sponsor of the iconic Rick and his Ramblers for over 25 years. He is an essential part of our community."

Harry Atkinson humorously echoed others' sentiments. "Rick provided a great variety of local musical talent at the festival and paid them well. All while driving Nash Ramblers that needed to have water added to the radiator every half mile, except for one '65 Ambassador convertible he drove which filled up to the bottom of the doors every time it rained and took two turns of the wheel to make the car steer in either direction!"

As Rick seasoned into a senior statesman of Vermont music, he greatly appreciated all the people here and abroad that kept in touch with him over the years. One fellow in particular was Hugh Aldous, the British folk club organizer who discovered Rick at the *Stevenage Folk Festival* in 1965. Hugh and his wife Nancy retired to the south of Spain years ago, and in 2010 decided to put together a small folk tour in honor of their original English folk club's 45th anniversary. Hugh contacted Rick through the Ramblers' website and invited him to come to Spain to be part of the celebration and to perform during a ten-day solo tour put together by Hugh and a local music agent.

Excited as he was at the kind invitation, Rick was a little nervous as it had been many years since he'd done an English-style folk club concert. He wanted to make sure he was up to the task so he put a couple sets of material together and invited a group of close friends to the Ranch for the first solo concert he'd done in Burlington in years. He set up for the show in his music room, the walls of which were lined with old instruments, gold records, concert posters, banners, and all kinds of Ramblers memorabilia. Even the actual sales rack from which Rick bought his first Elvis record in 1956 sat in a corner of the room. He had purchased the rack when Bailey's Music Rooms went of business in the 1980's. And though it was old and brittle, Rick's unique 18-string guitar stood proudly on a guitar stand by the door, the talisman he had carried with him for so long.

Rick assembled chairs for the concert on the rug that Hank Williams, Jr. played on as a boy and laid out a spread of crackers, wine and cheese. The room had warm lighting from several antique lamps which gave it an intimate feel. In the audience that evening was his old friend, Holly Miller, and her husband Bobby. She fondly remembered what it was like hearing Rick play in that special setting. "That night at his house concert before the Spain trip was amazing. When you walk into Rambler Ranch, you immediately feel the reverence Rick has for old things. His house is a sacred, comforting place; it has such a powerful, earthy presence you don't experience so much these days. Rick's life is truly a historical trail. Connecting people and preserving and promoting Vermont history through his music has been his life's purpose. Despite the very tough times he had with his family growing up at the Shelburne Museum, Rick was on fertile ground. He knew it and appreciated it."

Holly paused and smiled. "Around that time, one of my dear friends, Lois McClure, also visited Rambler Ranch with me and she got excited about the whole thing, the whole thing that is Rick."

Lois and her late husband, J. Warren ("Mac") McClure were longtime fans of Rick and the Ramblers, first hearing them at Holly and her husband, Bobby's birthday bashes at their Shelburne home. Rick's eyes lit up as he reminisced, "Whenever we played at the Miller's parties, Lois and Mac McClure were the first ones out on the dance floor. They were great fun and danced to just about every number. They were such classy, down-to-earth people; a great couple to have in your audience."

Mac McClure passed away years ago but Lois and Rick remained friends and she was very supportive of his musical projects over the years. She recently said of the Ramblers' front man: "I've always thought Rick Norcross was a gutsy guy, especially the way he can put things together."

The McClures had a long and rich history with Burlington and the steamboat *Ticonderoga*. Lois' father owned the *Burlington Free Press* in the 1930's and 1940's and he would commute from his lake home on Thompson's Point in Charlotte to the Burlington waterfront aboard the *Ti*, and then walk uptown to the *Free Press* offices. The *Ti* was an important presence in their lives as well as that of the whole Champlain region.

In the early 1950's, as a young man, Mac McClure was hired to work for the newspaper. After he moved to town, Mac met Lois, they fell in love, and he ended up marrying the boss's daughter. Mac worked his way up through the ranks, eventually becoming the publisher, before buying the paper with an investment group in 1961. After running the *Free Press* for ten years, the group sold it to the Gannet Company in 1971. In retirement, the McClures turned their attention to a life of philanthropy which benefited countless people from all over the region. One of their generous gifts was a donation of over a million dollars in 1992 to start a major and much needed restoration of the *Ticonderoga*.

Since that November day in 1954, when Rick and his family took the last voyage across Shelburne Bay, the *Ti* had suffered the sub-zero temperatures, brutal winds and deep snows of nearly 40 Vermont winters, as well as the beating sunshine and rainstorms of its summers. Her paint and trim and complex wooden structure had fallen into serious decay and without an extensive restoration the last of the Lake Champlain steamboats was in danger of being lost. With the generous help of the McClures, and the estate of Ralph Nading Hill, the historian for whom Rick's mother typed those long manuscripts, the restoration project got under way. By 1998, the complicated project was completed and the *Ti* had been restored to its original grandeur. That September, Rick produced the *Ticonderoga Party*, celebrating the unveiling of the *Ti's* restoration.

In May of 2010, after preparing his concert material, at age 65, Rick flew to Murcia, Spain, and joined Hugh Aldous and others for his first European tour since 1974. Hugh recalled, "Rick was a bit nervous as it had been over 30 years since he last performed over here as a solo singer, but he need not have worried as he was very well received wherever he performed and he brought back pleasant memories of times gone past." Rick had a wonderful time playing in Spain and it reassured him that he was still able to successfully perform solo and delight his audiences. It also reminded him of the critical importance of those early experiences performing in England and Europe that gave him the confidence and chutzpah to launch his long and successful career.

When Rick returned from Spain, he took time to reflect on how fortunate he had been to do what he loved for so long. Living on Lake Champlain and playing with the band of his dreams, Rick headed into *retirement* age with no thought of laying down his guitar. It was also the 25th anniversary of the last time he played in Tampa, so he thought it would be fun to return and perform a nostalgic solo show, as he had so many times in the past.

He contacted a woman who organized folk concerts in Tampa and booked a show at a local folk venue in March of 2011. He contacted many of his old friends in the Tampa area, including Frank Ross, from his days working at the *Tampa Times* and the *Florida State Fair*. He also connected with several of the musicians he used to play with including Bob Rippy, Captain Lewis, Steve Hill, and Buddy Klein, who was a frequent performer at Rick's Eighteenth String coffeehouse, and ran the club's Monday night *Hootenannies*, a popular *open mike* show.

Rick left for Tampa ahead of an early March snowstorm, just as he had in the mid Sixties. This time, however, he wasn't struggling along in one of his dilapidated farm trucks, but instead drove his comfortable convertible which, of course, had just had its engine rebuilt. The weather was beautiful when he arrived in Tampa and he enjoyed visiting several musician friends and some of his old haunts that were still standing. On the day of his concert, Rick displayed a collection of his classic Rock and Roll photographs on the walls of the venue. He was delighted to see in the audience a number of musicians that he had played with back in the 1970's and 1980's, including Bob Rippy, a world class lead guitarist, who spent years on the road touring out of Nashville with major national acts including Tommy Overstreet. Rippy had also played many times in Rick's bands both in Florida and at the *Chew Chew Festival* in Vermont.

Also in the audience that day was Captain Lewis, another Florida musician who was the house band leader at The Imperial Room in Tampa, a popular country music club that brought in major country acts that were backed by Lewis' band. Rick considered Captain Lewis a consummate keyboardist and sax player and feels fortunate to have had him play in his early Ramblers band when they performed at the *Florida State Fair*. In addition to continuing his long music career, Lewis is also well known for his beautiful ceremonial white dove releases. He raises his own flock of pure white doves on his Florida farm and performs the releases for all sorts of celebratory occasions and for free at memorial services for fallen soldiers and police officers.

On that warm Sunday afternoon in Tampa, Rick took the stage and pulled out a collection of Lake Champlain Chocolates he had brought with him from Vermont and personally passed one out to each member of the audience. Talk about Yankee hospitality! He then entertained an audience of new and old friends with his wonderful Vermont songs, including his very funny, recently penned tune about formaldehyde and flowers, entitled, "You Can't Make It Up," to which the crowd responded with laughter and applause. University of South Florida's college newspaper, *The Oracle*, sent a young student reporter to interview Rick and cover the show. That was a special experience for Rick as it was the same campus newspaper he wrote for and edited after Knocky Parker helped him transfer to USF in 1966. It was the student reporter's first article, so she was quite nervous and greatly appreciated not only Rick's outgoing and empathic demeanor but the wealth of material his life story had to offer.

After returning from Tampa, Rick started looking ahead to 2013, which would mark his 50th anniversary as a professional musician. He was also about to be embraced by a new extended family he met in a most unexpected way.

Chapter Twelve

A NEW FAMILY OF RAMBLERS

One of the biggest challenges of Rick's life was his tumultuous early years in Shelburne, which did not prepare him for enjoying close, ongoing family ties. Though he did briefly reconnect with his father off and on in the late 1960's, they never established a very meaningful relationship. Rick looked back on those days. "Due to the way I was brought up by my mother, I never developed very good negotiating skills or learned ways to talk things through with someone. That was something that made life as a kid in Shelburne tough and very lonely a lot of the time.

"Unfortunately, for much of my life I was the same way and about 25 years ago my father and I had a falling out over some trivial thing that I can't even remember. And like it was with my mother and her mother, I just stopped talking to him and we never spoke again." Rick shook his head. "It was immature and sad and I wish it hadn't been like that. I didn't even know when my father died. I still don't know exactly. Never went to a funeral or anything. The reality is I haven't had a very successful family life, at least as far as my nuclear family goes. Luckily I've had good relationships with my cousins and others from East Hardwick, and I still stay in touch with them on a fairly regular basis."

Though he had little to do with his mother after he left home at 16 and moved to East Hardwick, she and Rick eventually reconnected during his many years of traveling back and forth between Tampa and Vermont. She let him stay in a basement room in her Burlington house, sometimes for a month at a time while he was performing up north during the summer. She had long since left the Shelburne Museum and had finally retired after working for many years as a court reporter for the state.

"By the mid 1980's, my mother was living in a large house at North and Prospect Streets and soon after she retired — to her chagrin — my grandmother moved in with her. Ten long years later my grandmother died and my mother inherited a substantial amount of money from her. Then, as fate would have it in my family, two weeks later my mother was dragged down a flight of stairs by my half-brother's 80 pound basset hound. She wound up at Mary Fletcher Hospital and had a stroke as a result of the fall. When I went to visit her she was in bad shape and they didn't think she'd survive."

Rick's last memory of his mother is a painful one. Her dying words to him were, "I'm sorry." She was clearly carrying a burden, but he didn't know what she meant until later at the reading of her will when it was revealed that she had cut him entirely out of her estate. Rick was dumbfounded. "Ironically, my relationship with my mother had really improved in recent years. By then she had a real sense of humor, and we had a good friendship at the end. She even seemed happy with all that I'd done in music. I had no idea she had gotten upset and changed her will and that she would do that baffles me to this day. What hurt the most wasn't the loss of the inheritance, it was that my mother had never told me what she had gotten so upset about, thus we never had a chance to work it out."

Rick continued, "And then, to add insult to injury, other family members apparently felt badly about what she'd done so they said they'd give me ten percent of their inheritance. I thought that was nice, but they ultimately reneged so it felt like I got slapped twice over whole thing, especially since I had not asked for their donation."

Despite the painful family situations, looking back Rick describes his life as "a blessed miracle," largely because of the great friends that have so enriched his journey. Many of them are dedicated musicians that he has played and worked with over the years and others are special people who have deeply embraced him and his lifetime of playing music. One of those is his close friend of over 28 years, Dan Dubonnet, general manager of Vermont's largest group of commercial radio stations, including country music station, WOKO in Burlington.

Rick and Dan met in 1983, when he was an on-air personality for what was then WQCR radio. Dan was attracted to Rick's infectious enthusiasm as well as his witty, on-stage antics during his concerts. Dan also loved Rick's original Vermont songs and the danceable western swing music he had brought to northern New England. As Dan recalled, "We became friends and what impressed me about Rick Norcross the most back then – and still does – is what an authentic human being he is, totally dedicated to not only his own music, but to affording other musicians great opportunities to play. And he is a *great* song writer who has preserved a lot of important Vermont heritage in his work. He's like a musical 'for everyman' that writes and sings about things we all can relate to. Plus, he and the band are great fun to listen to. I assure you, they have never disappointed a crowd. Our station has taken great pleasure and pride in partnering with such a talented homegrown Vermont entertainer."

By the time Rick's band had morphed into the Ramblers, Dan signed WOKO on as a major sponsor for their summer tours around Vermont. In addition to their regular gigs, the band started performing at large concerts and events put on by the station, including six annual WOKO *Country Club Music Festivals*, which typically drew an audience of 10,000 from all over the North Country. The Ramblers performed on the bill with many top name national artists including Brad Paisley, Terri Clark, Lonestar, John Anderson, Jason Aldean, and Craig Morton.

Rick's respect and affection for Dan runs deep, "Dan's and WOKO's support of the Ramblers was instrumental in getting us off the ground and out there to a much larger audience. Over the years, he has been an unbelievable fan and I consider him and his wonderful family to be some of my most cherished friends. They have made me feel most welcome in their home for many years. Anyone who's been around me knows how much I like to eat, and I can tell you there's nothing quite like Christmas dinner at the Dubonnet's. They're some of the very special people that have given me the loving, funny family I never really had."

While Rick felt blessed to have so many good friends and fans, there was another local family that became a very special and integral part of the Ramblers family. In 1991, a young woman named Joan Shannon met Rick at an event when she was working for a local photographer. Many years later in 2007, Rick and Joan reconnected as Joan was the Burlington City Councilor that represented the district where Rick lived. At that time Rick was working to stop a new fire department ordinance charging events a separate fee for *every* tent set up on site, which would have been a huge financial burden to the *Chew Chew* and other Burlington festivals. Rick got in touch with Joan and solicited her help. After some discussion, he convinced her that the proposed ordinance didn't make sense, and she was able to get it amended. Rick was very appreciative and sent Joan and a few other city counselors his new CD, *I Rode the Ti*, as a thank you for their help.

By then, Joan was married to an engineer named Ken Grillo, and they had a beautiful young daughter named, Julia. Rick's *I Rode the Ti* CD sat around Joan and Ken's house unopened for several months then one day six-year-old Julia was in the kitchen listening to one of her father's "insufferable old albums" and decided she'd had enough. Several years later, Julia recalled that day. "I said to my dad, 'please turn this awful Janis Joplin music *off*. I can't take it anymore.' My mom heard what was going on and suggested I open up a new CD a friend had given her." Desperate for some new music, Julia tore the plastic off *I Rode the Ti*, and put it in their CD player.

Julia lit up with excitement when recalled the first time she heard Rick and his Ramblers singing western swing songs. "When I heard that song, 'Swing of the Range,' I thought it was *so* wonderful and a lot better than that Janis Joplin! I couldn't wait to play the CD over and over again." (Which her parents confirmed she did until, as her dad said, their ears were ready to bleed – but it was better than listening to Barney.) It just so happened "Swing of the Range" was a big song from the 1940 Gene Autry movie, *Rancho Grand,* sung by the young actress, Mary Lee, the same Mary Lee that had been Rick's mother's friend and neighbor at Fort Ethan Allen.

After playing *I Rode the Ti* incessantly for a week, Julia, then in first grade, was really curious about who this Rick guy was, so her parents let her e-mail him. Rick was delighted to hear from a young fan and invited her and her family over to visit Rambler Ranch. Julia's dad, Ken, comes from a musical family and was impressed with the high quality of the Ramblers' recording so he, too, was excited to meet Rick. When they arrived for their visit, Julia and her parents were fascinated by all the antiques and memorabilia that Rick had collected over the years. "It's really fun to be at Rick's Ranch," Julia says. "It's filled with neat stuff even though the place is really old. His front room has all kinds of colorful music banners hanging from the ceiling and over on the table is a wonderful old carnival machine that you put a coin in and a steam shovel-thing picks up a prize for you and you get to look at it."

Julia's eyes opened wide as she continued. "The most amazing thing Rick did was show me the *real* movie where Mary Lee is singing "Swing of the Range," including the yodeling part which I didn't know how to do. I always hated music class because it's not the real thing – people are just singing other peoples' songs – but Rick and his own band *are* the real thing and I love it."

Julia's mom remembered that day well. "When Rick showed her that movie clip it was like magic because I realized that somehow the two of them – despite their huge age difference – were on the same wavelength. And one of the things that really struck me was when we were driving home, Julia told us that the way Mary Lee sang the song in the movie was different than the way the Ramblers sing it on their *Ti* CD, including the fact that there were more verses.

We realized that she had carefully analyzed and memorized all the words and was working hard at singing it just the way it was on Rick's CD. She was *really* serious about it."

Rick quickly became part of the Shannon-Grillo's extended family and they began inviting him over for dinner during which, of course, he would always sing a couple of songs with Julia. When her seventh birthday rolled around, Julia decided to have a Mary Lee-themed party and Rick brought a whole collection of memorabilia out to their camp on Mallet's Bay and decorated it by hanging old Mary Lee movie posters on the walls. The kids all dressed up in cowgirl outfits and Ken found someone to come with their rather aged horse, "Sonny," to give the kids rides. Just as the party started, a thunderstorm struck and all 20 kids ended up inside the camp and "because the old horse wouldn't fit," Rick ended up taking over. A natural showman, he was able to keep them all entertained and in good spirits until the storm passed.

Joan speaks of the rather amazing relationship that developed between her family and Rick and between him and Julia in particular. "Rick has probably never had a relationship with a child — *ever*. His experience has been very limited, like not ever getting down on the floor and playing with a kid. So what happened when he and Julia met was that she came to where *he* was, not just to Rambler Ranch, but more importantly to his appreciation of music and they shared it from the beginning in a very adult way. He shared his deep love of music and history with her and she paid attention, soaked it up and responded by learning his songs very quickly and accurately and I think he had great respect for her doing that, especially at such a young age."

Around this time, Julia was with her parents at a district sailing regatta on Lake Champlain and during the entertainment portion of the program, Julia was asked to sing. Without hesitation, she got up and sang one of the Ramblers' songs — Patsy Cline's "Walking After Midnight" — which, according to her mother, she had been singing in the house non-stop for a couple of weeks. The audience loved her performance and she couldn't wait to tell Rick about it.

When he heard what she'd done, the seed was planted that there just might be a junior Rambler in the making.

In July of 2010, the Shannon-Grillos rode with the band on the *Pickle* to a show at Button Bay State Park. Even though Rick was hoping Julia might get up on stage and sing a song with them, Joan says he didn't really know how to go about asking her. So a member of the band, Juliette McVicker, kindly asked Julia to join the Ramblers on stage. Again, without hesitation, up she went and sang every word of the song. After her debut as a special guest singer, Julia's parents bought her a few western outfits and she has since performed with the band on multiple occasions and the audiences seem to love her.

Julia was ebullient when she talked about singing with the Ramblers. "I never get nervous up on stage because it's so much fun. And now I have my *own* mike stand because when I first sang with them I stood on a wooden box and got on my tiptoes to sing into Rick's microphone. I've even learned how to yodel on my favorite song."

Julia's first *professional* gig with the band was in the summer of 2011, when the scheduled female singer had to cancel out on the show. Julia was there but wasn't prepared to sing many of the Ramblers' songs, but Rick asked her if she would stand in anyway. She was excited at the opportunity though her mother was hesitant because Julia wasn't adequately prepared. Nonetheless, Joan supported her daughter wanting to sing and off they went to their car, slid Rick's CD into the player and listened carefully to the words of the songs Julia didn't know. A quick study, Julia listened intently, memorized the songs, and was soon on stage singing with her favorite band and never missed a note.

Julia beamed when she talked about that day. "That show was *so* exciting because these kids were dancing right down in front of the stage while I was singing and after the show they came running at me when I came off the stage. They were all around me, asking if I had my own CD and I didn't know what to say." Julia shook her head. "I thought to myself: this is what famous people must feel like and it must be frustrating for them." In addition to being a guest

Rambler, Julia shared with a grin that she has another part-time job when she's performing with the band. "Don't tell him, but sometimes Rick forgets a lyric to one of his own songs — like his most famous one, "I Rode the Ti," and my Dad tells me to mouth the words for Rick to help him out."

Julia's mom reflected on what meeting Rick has meant to their daughter and to their family. "What a chance Rick took the first time they brought Julia up on stage. Where else do you find a professional musician that would have enough faith and guts to put an eight-year-old on stage with a very well known band? And we love getting together on a regular basis, usually for a spaghetti dinner once a week, even if Rick and Julia sometimes make a mess. He always brings something over to the house, including his collection of Gene Autry and Mary Lee movies, which he and Julia love to watch together. They are quite a pair. We have all become close with Rick and appreciate that he is truly a special and unique part of Vermont history."

Julia's father, Ken agreed. "I think what brought us together is the great personal friendship we developed rather quickly. Rick is such a generous, thoughtful guy who loves to share what he loves with other people. With his original Vermont songs, he is making very important generational connections between people of all ages. He's a very special guy."

The friendship between Rick and the Shannon-Grillos deepened just before the fourth of July in 2010, when the Rambler's sound company abruptly quit. It happened just days before the band's annual Perkins Pier performance at the Burlington fireworks, and Rick didn't have a backup plan. He talked to Joan about it and she spontaneously volunteered that her recently retired, engineer husband would be "happy" to go out and buy a sound system and be ready for the fireworks show. Ken, being the great guy that he is, did just that, engineering a fine show, running his new system off the generator housed in the back of the *Pickle*. Many miles down the road, Ken is happily a permanent and invaluable part of the band, serving as both road manager and sound engineer.

As Rick's career approaches its half-century mark, he credited these and other close friends as having given him the support and enthusiasm to keep at it all these years. "Without these wonderful folks, I just wouldn't be here and neither would the band. And with Julia and other young kids who have become fans, we're seeing a new generation interested in this great amalgamation of music and the old fashioned fun that goes along with a western swing concert. It's really traditional family entertainment and it does my heart good to know that when I'm gone, I'm pretty sure the music will live on up here in the northern reaches." Rick smiled and shook his head. "It's just hard to believe how enthusiastic our fans have been over the years; like Elaine Russell and her entire family from Vergennes, who have rarely missed a show."

Though Harold Patch and his grandmother Delilah were long deceased, Rick kept in touch with folks in East Hardwick, the place he will always call home. He has generously helped raise money for local events and still reads the *Hardwick Gazette* from cover to cover every week. To show appreciation for Rick, in May of 2011, the town asked him to be the "Celebrity Master of Ceremonies" for the *Hardwick Spring Festival* parade, exactly 50 years after he first performed in what was then known as the *Tulip Festival.* Hardwick had witnessed one of their own go out onto the world stage and they were grateful he brought the benefits of what he learned back home.

Despite the many roads he traveled and the tremendous changes in his life, Rick's heart and soul never changed. As Becky Blanchard, his eighth grade teacher poignantly said, "From the time he was a little kid in my classroom, Rick has been a thoroughly authentic human being, and at 68, he's just as curious about discovering life and people and the good in both as he was back then. He has always stayed focused and never gotten lost like so many other artists. With all he's been through, he is still remarkably thankful for everything he has, and I don't mean monetary things. I think this is why so many people have been attracted to Rick over the years, from the 'lowly' local to some of the most famous singers of the century. His life has always been about the journey, not fame and fortune, and –" she adds with a chuckle, "he sure hasn't had much of the latter!"

As Rick looked ahead to his upcoming anniversary, there were two things in particular that were gnawing on him. One was the sad condition of the *Pickle* and the realization that its deteriorating body wasn't going to hold together to make his 2013 tour. While Rick maintained "she ran like a watch," too many Vermont winters had taken a toll on the paint which was peeling and the sheet metal and supports underneath which were rusting badly. Rick desperately wanted to preserve this special piece of Americana but it was financially far beyond his or the Ramblers' reach.

The second concern was "after twenty-odd years of hard playing, the D-45 Wonder Guitar was just plain worn out." Unable to be played, Rick had put his trusty guitar away, seemingly for good, though it pained him not to perform with it during his anniversary.

So, in true Norcross fashion, Rick put his fundraising energies into high gear to save the band's beloved *Pickle* and get her in shape for his upcoming tour. And with the encouragement of Ken Grillo, Rick contacted a fellow named Dave Nichols, a master luthier at Custom Pearl Inlay in Waddington, New York, who agreed to perform a complete restoration of the guitar in time for the 2013 tour. Saving the Pickle, however, would turn out to be much more of a challenge.

Chapter Thirteen

A *PICKLE* PARTY

To save the Ramblers' bus, Rick organized the "Preserve the Pickle" fund-raising campaign, which included a colorful, eye-catching brochure which he mailed to several hundred of the band's longtime supporters. He called it, "our first-ever and last-ever public appeal for support." In addition to the mailing, Rick thought it would be fun to hold a *Pickle Party*, both to have an afternoon of great music and to help raise money through a silent auction. His faithful friend and supporter, Dan Dubonnet, enthusiastically got on board and Burlington's independent newspaper, *Seven Days*, helped drum up interest by running a great article about Rick and the *Pickle* restoration written by Matt Bushlow.

On a warm, sunny afternoon in April of 2012, the extended Ramblers family gathered at Burlington's St. John's Club. Parked right in front of the club was the Ramblers' beloved, but badly rusted, *Pickle*. Originally built as an intercity bus by the Flxible coach company in 1957, this particular Starliner model was unique as it had a raised roof with an observation window for the comfort and enjoyment of its passengers. In 1961, long before Rick bought it, the bus was purchased by a wealthy businessman who transformed it into a luxury motor coach, complete with custom woodwork, Naugahyde upholstery and air conditioning. The bus slept six, had a lounge in the rear, a full galley, rest room with shower, and comfortably seated fourteen.

The *Pickle* has been on the road for 55 years, since 1998 with the Ramblers. It has also served as a classic backstage respite for WOKO's many *Country Club Music Festivals* and for Shelburne Museum's *Concerts on the Green*. It has been visited by superstars from Miranda Lambert to John Fogerty and the bluegrass group, The Seldom Scene. The iconic *Pickle* has appeared in two movies filmed in Montreal, one of which starred Jennifer Love Hewitt. It also appeared in several episodes of the TV show, *Entertainment Tonight,* and in 2004, was the tour bus for Burlington Mayor Peter Clavelle's campaign for governor. "The *Pickle* just seems to attract everyone," Rick said with admiration. "She's got a special magnetism."

By the time the Ramblers took the stage that Sunday afternoon, the St. John's Club was buzzing with supporters who munched on – of course – fresh dill pickles, while they enjoyed the spectacular view looking out over a placid Lake Champlain to the Adirondack Mountains of New York. The crowd was entertained by a wonderful gathering of musicians including a guest performance by Rick's longtime friend and collaborator, LeRoy Preston, who sang several of his megahits including, "My Baby Thinks She's A Train," and "Route 66."

Rick is widely respected for his ability to bring together musicians and audiences from many different backgrounds. To that end, another pair of performers at the *Pickle Party* was a hot new jazz duo in town named, Dwight and Nicole. Backed by the Ramblers, they took the stage and put on a smokin' set that got the place rocking so much security had to shut the doors so as not to bother the neighbors. Incidentally, later that year, the very talented Nicole Nelson was a contestant on NBC TV's program, *The Voice.*

During the *Pickle Party,* a silent auction featured many great items including a private gourmet dinner by Vermont chef, James MacPherson, several interesting antiques, jugs of maple syrup, gift certificates to area stores and a beautiful handmade onyx lamp by Burlington artisan, Dave Ashworth. At the end of the afternoon, the crowd was on their feet cheering all the musicians and support people who made the day possible including Ken Grillo, who did a superb job engineering the sound and his wife, Joan Shannon, who oversaw the auction. And at Rick's invitation, their songstress daughter, Julia, took the stage and beautifully sang one of her favorite Patsy Cline songs, "Walking After Midnight." Performing with Julia, it is obvious that Rick takes great pleasure in helping pass the torch of Mary Lee's impassioned swing-style singing to another beautiful and talented young performer.

"What a blast!" bass player, Dave Rowell said after the last note was played. Dave comes from a multi-generational farm family from East Craftsbury, and has played in Vermont bands for over 30 years, including the well known WDEV Radio Rangers. He joined the Ramblers five years ago and his respect for the band's leader runs deep. "It is great playing with Rick, who has such a fun demeanor. He's a real generous soul who loves to perform and make people feel good and is always very appreciative of the musicians he plays with. He's also a very good writer who's never afraid to try new things. Rick is steeped in history but his original songs are truly new music that connects people to the importance of the past, which means a lot to me." He laughed. "Just take a look at that big *Pickle* parked outside."

Dave continued, "Though Rick grew up in the middle of dairy farm country, he knew early on that he had better things to do than be married to a cow. He's so important because he has an accumulated history that no one else is aware of; a story no one else can tell and he does it so well in his songs. In the years ahead, I am really looking forward to bringing his music to new venues that haven't heard Rick or the Ramblers yet. There's nothing like springing western swing on unsuspecting audiences."

Brett Hoffman, the Ramblers' drummer, is also very appreciative of being in one of Vermont's premier bands. "Ramblers gigs are always great fun, especially when you get to play with legends like Rick and LeRoy Preston. When

I joined the band, I knew I was playing for a Vermont institution and after a few years on the road with Rick and this bunch of crazy characters, I *feel institutionalized!*" Brett lives over in Newark in the Northeast Kingdom and says he often spends twice as much time on the road getting to and from shows as he does actually playing at them. "But it's way worth it," he said. "There's nobody else out there like Rick Norcross. It's like playing in a part of ongoing history."

Also in the back of the hall was a big fellow in a black cowboy hat named Bear Bessette, owner of Wildcat Busing in Hardwick. Bear was the brave man who took on the challenging task of restoring the *Pickle's* decaying bodywork. In between songs at the *Pickle Party*, Rick called out to Bear from the stage — as he often does — and thanked him for taking on the daunting task. Bear saluted the crowd with his long neck beer and many wished him good luck.

A few days after the *Pickle* benefit, Rick fired up the bus and headed to Hardwick, driving the same winding road along the Lamoille River that he and his family used to travel in the 1950's when he and his sister drove his mother crazy jumping up and down on the front seat. Rick felt a sweet nostalgia as he drove the pickle into Hardwick. Several old friends waved to him as he took a tour through town on his way to Bear's garage on the outskirts of the village. The next day, Bear's talented crew started tearing the bus apart — literally — finding layers of decayed metal underneath the rusted outer panels. With Bear's deep commitment to the project, new metal panels were cut and shaped to match the smooth curves of the Starliner. Over the next eight months, Bear's crew put in long hours, welding and grinding, then sanding and painting the bus, carefully restoring it to its former glory.

It was also in the spring of 2012, that Rick was contacted by Radio Vermont owner, Ken Squier, who asked if he would do a stint providing music and commentary for his radio stations' Saturday morning program, *The Radio Vermont Jamboree*. Rick was delighted and each week for the next three months featured Ramblers' songs on the *Jamboree*, producing and recording the show in the very same studio from which Harold Patch broadcast his folk music show back in 1936.

Ken Squier is not only a legendary broadcaster, he is also known nationwide as "The Voice of Nascar," due to his long-running association with racing, including many years calling races on CBS TV. Ken spoke of his friend with admiration. "Rick Norcross is a self-made man hewn out of all that makes Vermont so unique. Somehow over the decades he has carved out a music career which stays close to its roots in the music he composes, sings and plays. So often his work provides a sense of where he's from and what he has picked up traveling his own path, always bringing it back to the home place. You hear it whether on a recording, at a concert, or just a kitchen tunk over at the neighbors. Good on ya', Rick, good on ya'."

During the summer of 2012, Rick and his road manager, Ken, drove to upstate New York to pick up his restored D-45 guitar. Rick was thrilled to get his "Wonder Guitar" back. "Master luthier, Dave Nichols, had done a simply splendid restoration, turning my old worn out guitar into a masterpiece of quality with an amazing sound." His favorite guitar back in hand, Rick proceeded to write several new songs in preparation for recording his 50th Anniversary CD. That summer he also had a delightful visit from his old British friends, Hugh and Nancy Aldous, who came from their home in Spain for a two week visit at the beginning of July. They were thrilled to hear Rick and his Ramblers perform on Perkin's Pier just before Burlington's fireworks display. After the concert, Rick, the band and his friends retired to nearby Rambler Ranch and reminisced about the great times they'd shared in England. Hugh and Nancy also marveled at what Rick was still doing.

On his visit to Vermont, Hugh brought with him the original hand-written ledger from his "Clangers" folk club that lists all the gigs Rick and other musicians played in 1965. It includes the evening of November 26th when Rick played just before Doc Watson performed. Rick was paid two pounds Sterling ($2.80 US) for his performance that night, Doc received thirty pounds

($42 US), and it cost Hugh's folk club one pound to rent the hall and two pounds to lodge the performers for the night.

Hugh sat on Rick's balcony looking out over the lake and reflected. "It is just terrific to be here and see what a beautiful place Rick calls home and to know that he is still playing his music after all these years. He has had an extraordinary life with a hugely positive influence on so many, and Nancy and I are very grateful to still be a part of it. I hope people understand what an important figure Rick is on both sides of the Atlantic."

Another fellow who kindly reminisced about Rick was former British booking agent, Derek Sarjeant, who befriended Rick in his early London days. "Although Rick's material and style have changed over the many years I've known him, his voice is unmistakably recognizable – warm with a lovely mellow vibrato. He has made a unique contribution, and Rick can be justly proud of his 50 years contributing to the music world."

During the year, Rick worked on many new songs for the Ramblers' upcoming CD, including "Don't Make Me Beg," a song he wrote with his keyboard player, Charlie MacFadyen. It was the first time Rick had ever written a song with a band member and it was a real thrill for him. It was also clear that Charlie has thoroughly enjoyed his years as one of the Ramblers. "What I respect most about Rick is his strong sense of community and music's role in bringing people together. He cares deeply about his fellow musicians and about each and every person sitting in the audience. I've taken many a ride in Rick's bus to gigs, and he's full of stories, which find their way into his songs. Anyone who listens to our new CD will immediately appreciate how Rick can tell a funny story about a place like Hardwick, while at the same time expressing his true love for the town and its people."

In December, Rick and the band hunkered down at Lane Gibson Recording Studios in Charlotte, Vermont, and amongst the usual hilarity, began recording tracks for their new CD, *Riding My Guitar*, which featured eight new songs that Rick wrote for his anniversary. After the recording sessions, Rick sat behind the control panel carefully listening to a take of a new, Hardwick-based song entitled, "You Can't Make it Up." A subtle smile appeared on his face as he sang along with the lyrics which relate his experiences at Hardwick Academy in the 1960's, where the only place you could get flowers for the high school prom was from Holcomb's Funeral Home, the local undertaker. As LeRoy Preston said, "At heart, Rick is a real folk artist and a great song writer. That song is what you call 'original material.' Not everyone can perfectly write and deliver a hysterical formaldehyde song right out of East Hardwick."

The song goes like this,

I'll tell you a story and I swear that it's true
about Hardwick Academy in 1962
The Junior Prom "Where Dreams Come True" came along that year
I asked a classmate to the dance, I overcame my fear
Harold Holcomb's Funeral Home's the only place in town
where you could buy fresh flowers to pin upon her gown
You had to call the week before to order in advance
and then you'd pick your corsage up and take it to the dance
Downstairs in one big cooler they kept everything inside
The dead, the flowers that they sold and the formaldehyde
It didn't matter to the dead, they have no sense of smell
the flowers in the cooler looked like heaven smelled like hell
Midnite by Tussy on the girls, the boys all wore Old Spice
but those flowers from the cooler didn't smell that nice
The overwhelming "eau de pew" rising like the tide
wafting from corsages was all formaldehyde
You pinned the corsage to her dress or tied it to her wrist
and when you danced a slow dance it was rising like the mist
But dancing to Ray Hussey's Band and holding your girl tight
everything was A-OK on that very special night
Today I go to funerals that familiar smell surrounding

I look into the casket and it sets my heart a-pounding
It's amazing how formaldehyde still makes me feel romance
it takes me back to Junior Prom and makes me want to dance
You can't make it up, you can't live it down
That's just the way things happen in this Northeast Kingdom Town
Hills of solid granite sometimes have a crack
Things that happened long ago, they're never coming back

As Rick listened to the song track, he was well aware of the amazing road he had traveled to get to that moment; the years of hard work and slim hope that he hung onto and the many kind-hearted friends that believed in him when he was just learning how to believe in himself. He wished Harold Patch could be there to listen to the wonderful sounds coming from the studio and see the members of his beloved band hamming it up in between takes, including ten-year-old Julia, harmonizing with Taryn Noel.

And next to Rick sat Ken, his close friend, road manager and sound man.

Rick spoke of his feelings. "Really, now my only goal is to make it through my 50th anniversary tour so I can pay homage to all the great folks who have made my life possible. Think of it – a kid from East Hardwick being lucky enough to live the life I've lived. It's a blessed miracle. The only other thing I would love is that after I'm gone, someone picks up and sings some of my original songs to keep them alive. That would be way cool."

Rick has made a positive and indelible impression on so many people over his long career. Perhaps folk singer, Carolyn Hester summed it up best. Looking back over their 50 years of friendship, she had this to say. "Each person in this world has a list of *The Unforgettables*, and Rick Norcross is one of mine. He is the 'Pied Piper of Vermont,' a fabulous talent who is always positive and looking ahead. He is also very realistic in matters of life as well as the arts. Many years ago when I had a bad case of the blues, he didn't hesitate to offer all the sympathy and understanding of a best friend. He was a 'Gentle Giant' to the rescue. Rick Norcross has entertained us all royally, just like he has lived his life…with gusto."

Perhaps what attracts people from so many different walks of life to Rick are his *everyman* qualities. Mingling and playing with the world's greatest stars, Rick always maintained a down-to-earth authenticity people can relate to. Through the legacy of his original songs, he has chronicled our own stories, regardless of where we come from. Whether he's singing about love found or lost, finding a way to scrape by, or enjoying the freedom of the open road or a magnificent lake, he invites us to travel with him.

Unlike with Elvis or other superstars, we mere mortals can actually imagine and relate to Rick's life and all that he has done. He is not out of reach; in fact, he is very much one of us, steeped in the same daily struggles we all deal with. Through his music he takes us along on his remarkable journey. His ability to form and maintain close, trusting friendships – particularly with other musicians – has been paramount to his success. As the Legendary Panama Red said, "Many years have gone by, but through those years, in my mind Rick Norcross remains a friend as constant as the North Star."

As Rick headed into 2013, he and his band were looking forward to playing some special gigs during his anniversary year, including the famed "Farmers Night" held in the ornate House Chamber at the Vermont State Capital in January. They would also play a concert for the Island Arts organization on the lawn of the beautiful Grand Isle Lake House in June, and their 24th annual Fourth of July show before the Burlington fireworks celebration.

After the countless miles he's traveled, on New Years Eve, Rick began celebrating his 50th anniversary as a singer-songwriter by performing a solo show at Burlington's *First Night* celebration. In many ways he had returned to the musical roots first put down in East Hardwick when he was a boy of just sixteen. Alone on a stage with his guitar and a song, Rick Norcross was back home again.

A PERSONAL NOTE FROM RICK

"Riding My Guitar for 50 years and more
It's taken me to places I'd have never gone before
Who'd have ever thought that it would go this long or far
I've had such a good time Riding My Guitar"

"It's all about the Music, it's all about the songs
It's all about the friends of ours who came to sing along
It's all about the Rambers, about the Pickle too
It's all about the songs we play and what they say to you"

As I head full tilt into my 50th year as a performing musician, my main feeling is one of profound gratitude. Gratitude for the friends that music has brought into my life. Gratitude for the wonderful places I have traveled to play music and for the many kindnesses extended to me by folks who have embraced my songs. Working on my biography with Steve brought back many forgotten memories and recollections of a long life spent making and listening to music. Most musicians don't get an opportunity to play out for as many years as I have and for that I am also incredibly grateful. Working below the radar of commercial success in the music business has given me the freedom to pick and choose my projects and audiences, another very rare luxury. I must also affirm my heartfelt thanks to those businesses and friends who have chosen to sponsor my bands and my projects, again allowing me to follow my dream. And I must tell you how proud I am of my band, The Ramblers. I always get to honestly say, this is the best band I ever had and this time, it's still *so true!* I am blessed to get to play with this exceptional (and wacky) group of Vermont musicians. Please go to our web site and meet them. Better yet, I invite each and every one of you to come out to hear us live someplace in Vermont on our "Riding My Guitar Tour" so that I can thank you in person for helping me to keep playing music for 50 years and more!"...*Rick Norcross, Rambler Ranch, Burlington, VT*

To order CD's, book the band for a special event, or to learn more about Rick and his Ramblers, please visit their website, www.rickandtheramblers. com.

213

ABOUT THE AUTHOR

Stephen Russell Payne is a fourth generation Vermonter from the Northeast Kingdom town of St. Johnsbury. Inspired during a visit to his seventh grade English class by Sheffield poet, Galway Kinnell, Payne has been writing ever since. He has published many stories, both fiction and non-fiction in *Vermont Life Magazine, the Tufts Review, Vermont Literary Review, Route 7 Literary Journal,* and others. Payne's first novel, *Cliff Walking* was published in 2011 to excellent reviews. Payne has made many appearances in support of the novel and to raise awareness and funds for organizations working to end spousal and child abuse, particularly, *Prevent Child Abuse Vermont.*

Payne is a graduate of Tufts University where he studied pre-med and English, receiving his Masters in English in 1978. He attended medical school and completed his surgical training at the University of Vermont College of Medicine, where he has been a Clinical Assistant Professor of Surgery since 1988. He practices general surgery in St. Albans, Vermont, where he lives on an organic farm with his family. Payne spends as much time as possible on Lake Champlain and is a strong supporter of *The Lake Champlain Land Trust,* as well as *The Vermont Land Trust.*

Stephen Russell Payne's debut novel, *Cliff Walking* is available at bookstores, on line through Amazon.com as a book or Kindle ebook, and through BarnesandNoble.com. More information is available at the author's website: www.StephenRussellPayne.com.

STEPHEN RUSSELL PAYNE

CLIFF
WALKING

A Novel

"Stephen Russell Payne has emerged as a new voice in Vermont's
impressive pantheon of creative writers, and a powerful one."
–Howard Frank Mosher

21202031R00135

Made in the USA
Charleston, SC
11 August 2013